Tim Costello was born in Melbourne on 4 March 1955 and was educated there—not least by lively family debate on politics and theology—until graduating in Law at Monash University in 1978. In 1979 he married Merridie and, after practising as a solicitor in family and criminal law, in 1981 Tim and Merridie both travelled to Switzerland to study theology, returning to Australia in 1984.

Ordained a Baptist Minister in 1987, the Reverend Tim Costello rebuilt the congregation at the St Kilda Baptist Church, opened a drop-in centre and started a legal practice for those for whom the law is normally inaccessible. Since 1988 he has also lectured part-time at Whitely Baptist Seminary in Melbourne. As elected Mayor of St Kilda Council in 1993, he became prominent for his championing of local democracy. In 1995 he became Director of the Urban Mission Unit for the Collins Street Baptist Church, which runs a refuge and outreach for homeless youth in Melbourne's city centre.

In recent years Tim Costello has also led the Interchurch Gambling Taskforce, has advised bankers on ethics, was elected a representative for The Real Republic ticket at the 1998 Constitutional Convention and was voted by the National Trust as one of Australia's 100 National Living Treasures. He is often called upon to address schools and community organisations and to comment on public issues for the media. He continues to live in St Kilda with his wife, who is a school chaplain, and his three children. When not involved with church and community activism, or writing, he enjoys reading, political and theological debate, films, basketball and football.

Tim Costello's previous publications are, as editor, *Ministry in an Urban World* (Acorn, Melbourne, 1991) and *Planning Legislation and Affordable Housing* (Vic Council of Churches, 1991).

streets of Hope

Finding God in St Kilda

TIM COSTELLO

ALLEN & UNWIN

AND

ALBATROSS BOOKS

First published in 1998 by
Allen & Unwin
9 Atchison Street
St Leonards NSW 1590
Australia
Phone: (61 2) 8425 0100
Fax: (61 2) 9906 2218
E-mail: frontdesk@allen-unwin.com.au
Web: http://www.allen-unwin.com.au

Albatross Books
PO Box 320, Sutherland NSW 2232
Australia
Fax: (61 2) 9521 1515
Email: albatross@albatross.com.au
Web: http://www.publishaustralia.com.au

National Library of Australia
Cataloguing-in-Publication entry:

Costello, Tim, 1955– .
Streets of Hope: finding God in St Kilda.

Includes index.
ISBN 1 86448 890 5.

1. Costello, Tim, 1955– . 2. St Kilda Baptist Church (St Kilda, Vic.).
3. Baptist Union of Australia—Clergy—Biography. 4. City churches—
Victoria—Melbourne. 5. City clergy—Victoria—Melbourne—Biography.
6. Community. 7. Inner cities—Victoria—Melbourne. I. Title.

286.194092

Set in 12/15pt Caslon 540 by DOCUPRO, Sydney
Cover and text design by Ruth Grüner
Cover image by Manuela Hoefer/The Photo Library
Author photograph by Jaime Murcia
Printed by Griffin Press Pty Ltd, South Australia

5 7 9 10 8 6

To Merridie, my companion on the journey

To our children: Claire, Elliot and Martin . . .
'May hope be there to meet you'

To all those who shared with us the experience of being
'Committed at the core and open at the edges'

contents

Preface

I finished writing this book in 1995, after my ministry and engagement in local politics in St Kilda, and before I became the minister at Collins Street Baptist Church in the centre of Melbourne. It is a highly personal story of my journey up until 1994, which I wrote partly in order to answer the questions that arose wherever I spoke, about what shaped me and my values. In fact, the very process of writing this book served as a 'therapy' for me: four years ago, it helped me to see more clearly where I stood.

Since this book was written, my thoughts have undergone a good deal of development as I have tackled the issues that a city church confronts. In my immediate city parish is the Victorian Parliament, the Stock Exchange, the massive Crown Casino, and a cross-section of people from CEOs to the street people who became my friends in St Kilda. My formative experiences in the years described in this book remain with me as my source of wisdom and inspiration for ministry, even if the context has changed. Much of what I describe about my ministry in St Kilda continues in some shape or form, although, naturally, faces and programs differ. Change assaults us on every front in life and little is left unaffected by it. The question facing us all is how community and values survive in the post-modern rapids of our time.

When my term as Mayor of St Kilda was drawing to a close in 1994, I decided against an offer of a safe Senate seat with the Democrats in order to be less public and more focussed in ministry. The irony is that I have found myself increasingly addressing political, social and moral issues. The area of prophetic engagement and public articulation of values is seen by some as inherently political. Does this not contravene Church/State separation and risk spiritual compromise? These are among the broader questions that I want to pursue in a further book; for now, this one is offered as a sketch of the journey that has shaped my faith and values, and to help contextualise my public statements and articles.

This book was also written to challenge the Church. Many will find its language and categories a tad religious. However, I do not draw hard boundaries between the sacred and the secular, and hope that the discerning reader may recognise the passion for holism even if the religious concepts are unfamiliar. It is this lack of boundaries between Bible and newspaper, prayer and politics that continues to define my worldview and undergirds my passion for life. Indeed, it is only at the intersection of what you think you believe and how you ultimately live that you come to discover what is true faith. Spirituality is the consistent application of one's values.

Tim Costello
March 1998

Introduction

People's needs, I have come to believe, are best served in the context of community. Community has always fascinated me. We live out our lives under the gaze and influence of others and learn much about ourselves from those who make up our world. Community is found in our families, the neighbourhood, school, church and workplace.

This book is about a few of the different communities I have known—about the way they have served my needs and the way they have served the needs of others. More particularly, the communities I am looking at are: Blackburn, where I grew up, a community bound together by homogeneity; Switzerland, where I studied theology, a country where the community is tightly organised and self-protective; Eastern Europe under communism, where communities were bound together by a fear of the State; and, most fully, St Kilda, where I worked for ten years, a series of particular cultural communities united by an ethic of tolerance and diversity.

This is also a story of integration. In a world where specialisation is supreme, I have tried to interface the areas of law, Church, local government, community and family. Specialists in each of these areas may smile condescendingly at my naiveties. Professions, by definition, intend to be accessible only to professionals. The institutions of Church, law, social work and community development, and government have all developed a conceptual base and framework known as, respectively, theology, jurisprudence, sociology and political philosophy. The expertise developed in each of these fields is to serve the public. But the sophistication of ideas and the parallel sophistication of language locks out many of those most affected by these autonomous domains. Consequently, people remain dependent on the professions, silenced by their impenetrable definitions of reality.

We face the disintegration of a cohesive culture and watch somewhat helplessly as it is refracted through retribalised subcultures. It is a time for integration; the putting together into a whole.

Integrity is a magnificent personal characteristic and derives from the idea of integration. To live with integrity means to put together the component parts. For me it means to relate worship and politics, prayer and economics, social justice in the family and on the international stage. Too many marriages have been destroyed by one partner's passionate and perceptive vision regarding global inequities and total blindness to spouse, parenting and family inequities. Integrity is justice and mercy kissing; it is the material finding its place in harmony with the spiritual, not replacing it.

I have chosen to tell the story of integration without any apologies for the personal nature of this story. It is not intended as an autobiography, but more a diary of observation of the struggle to build an integrated model of community. Not all will agree with the generalisations that flow from these observations and some will feel there are unfair caricatures. This is expected, as we all see the same events and the same world according to the tint of the spectacles we have chosen. It is hard to say anything unless some licence in generalities and arbitrary interpretations from anecdotes encrust around the underlying truths. The master storyteller, Jesus of Nazareth, demonstrated that we each have to work out the open-ended meaning of his parables by living them. Only then do we occupy them for ourselves. Doctrine, dogma and propositions impart narrow-minded security, but not truth. I also have chosen to tell the story through the eyes of those who formed our community, many in the underbelly of Australian society.

What follows is an attempt to name and oppose the forces of fragmentation that are assailing family, community, law, Church and government. I believe that as a Western culture we have consistently chosen prosperity and consumption before community, belonging and friendship. We have largely opted for competition, not cooperation. Fragmentation, not integration, results. The sense of fragmentation features in our transience. We are a nation on the move, increasingly unwilling or unable to put down solid roots in one place.

Fragmentation and transience are strong forces driven by a cancerous individualism that translates into a perverse public ethic. It teaches that if we all act selfishly in our own private consumerist interests, then society as a whole is benefited. This is ennobled by an appeal to a vague communal ethic of bequeathing to our children a higher standard of living than the one we received.

I agree that we should all try and leave the world a better place, but that is a far cry from handing on a more luxurious living standard which assumes inevitable growth and inexhaustible resources. That is a destructive myth, and it is time to rewrite the myth to assist us to live with less and to applaud lower standards of living. Lesser consumerist demands may permit fewer trees to be cut down, greater sharing of cars, less pollutants and a simpler lifestyle, so that others both now and in the future can simply live.

This is a story of trying to build community through the family, through the Church, through law and through local government. Holding them together to serve each other is my challenge to live with integrity.

Community is a threatened entity. Community groups are under threat because there are so few volunteers. Service clubs, churches, political parties, unions—and, in fact, any voluntary groups that require commitment—are struggling to hold members. People still expect voluntary auxiliaries like service clubs, churches and community groups to help them, and they can get quite angry if these agencies are not there for them in time of need. But there seem to be far more takers and far fewer joiners.

For so many, a fragmentation of beliefs and morals is the greatest source of confusion. When everything is *relative* it seems hard to know what to *absolutely* tell one's children. With endemic family breakdown, old-time family values seem *passé*. Ethical behaviour and morals appear stuck in constantly shifting sands, with the wheels rusting off. A consensus about 'right thinking' is ever so ambiguous and suffers death from a thousand qualifications. Our children know so much of the world's mess through television and grow up trying to make sense of far-reaching complexities like Rwanda, Bosnia and Timor that we adults cannot make sense of. They know all about their fundamental rights much younger than we did and so we start treating them as little adults much earlier.

All this spells pain for parents. Better information does not necessarily lead to better human formation. Fantastic communications technology does not lead to better communication.

More technologically sophisticated funparks do not lead to more freedom and fun. We yearn for simpler, clearer times when we knew that relationship, faith and love were the keys. Now the keys are comparative advantage and competitive edge. Hugh McKay charts it brilliantly in his social survey *Reinventing Australia: The Mind and Mood of Australia in the 90s*. He notes the widespread longing to find our bearings and get back to basics. This book is about such an attempt.

I tell the story from the position of one with faith. Why people believe is almost as mysterious as why some are born with white or black skin. Many raised in families where there is devout faith reject it later in life as a fantasy for the weak. Others who have no family history of devotion find to their surprise that they cannot but believe. In any event, it is where I plant my feet, where I find a place to stand and the perspective from which I live, work and draw my being.

The streets, sex and spirituality

My first legal client in St Kilda, in March 1985, was a sex worker named Julie. She arrived at St Kilda Baptist Church, which surprising as it might sound, houses a legal office, five minutes before her case was due to start at the St Kilda Court. She had made no appointment and her case was listed for that morning. I was going to discover that diaries and professional appointments were not the way St Kilda worked.

I hurriedly threw on my coat and we started walking to the old St Kilda Court, which was virtually at the end of the street where the church and legal office were located. I could not help noticing that she was sporting an ugly black eye, with bruising extending down over the cheekbone and towards her chin. I thought she had been callously bashed. I was wrong.

I asked her cautiously and sympathetically how she had received the bruising. Julie bluntly told me that her nerves had got to her the previous night when she realised that she might go to prison because of her many prior convictions for theft and prostitution, and so she had attempted to shoot up in her arm. After a number of failed attempts to locate a vein, she had got angry, and in desperation had injected heroin into a vein in her cheek. I inwardly freaked, but tried to look unshocked. As we kept walking, I started to wonder if I was cut out for work in such extreme subcultures.

We got to the court and waited around for most of the morning before the case was finally called. My plea in mitigation of the offence convinced the magistrate to give her one more chance before prison and he imposed yet another fine. Julie was ecstatic and told me indelicately how many clients it would take to pay out the fine. I was beginning to learn that this was a culture where money was not the unit of measurement, but where clients and packets of heroin defined the nature of commerce. She planted a big kiss on my cheek and graciously invited me out for lunch. I must confess to some deep-seated, middle-class ambivalence, and I hesitated before accepting.

Was this a smart way, in the eyes of the local traders, to start a respectable career as the local lawyer and minister of religion? But then I thought, Well, I cannot lie—I have not had any other offers for lunch today. And so I agreed and asked where we would dine. I was just a wee bit intrigued as to her preference in cafés. She replied with delight that she knew a soup kitchen down the road that provided a great free lunch.

So I walked with her the half-kilometre or so to the Roman Catholic Church's free-lunch program. Like a tourist in town, I was given a crash course in survival skills on the way. The walk took us through the heart of St Kilda's notorious redlight section. She showed me her beat and where one of her friends was bashed the week before. No, her friend hadn't reported the assault because last time she did, the police had just laughed and said, 'Show us your tits,' before kicking her out. I expressed disbelief that the police acted like that and she confirmed what I was later to discover is a prevalent cynical was a prostitute. Claire was curious and wanted the title explained. It's a person who lets others pay them for sex, she was told. Claire mused for a while and then added, 'So how do people know they are prostitutes? Do they wear a letter P or something?'

Well, there are no letter P's in St Kilda, but there is certainly a common look, stance, manner and even placement in the suburb that gives the intent away. St Kilda still is the main drag strip for street walkers in the Victorian capital.

St Kilda, the old tart of Melbourne

ᴧ

Whilst our city took its name from a clipper called the *Lady of St Kilda* that moored offshore in 1841, the city was to develop a reputation as less of a lady and more as the tart of Melbourne. Street prostitution has been a stubborn social reality for more than a century in St Kilda.

Mind you, it was not always like this. St Kilda of the 1880s was home to some of Melbourne's most prestigious families. The prices houses were fetching in the 1880s have never been equalled since in real terms. So when a prostitute was found in Acland Street, St Kilda, in 1886, the burghers were profoundly shocked and she was run out of town. St Kilda was declared most emphatically not to be a suitable place for such low types.

However, in 1912 the advent of Luna Park's thrill rides rendered St Kilda the cradle of popular entertainment. The spin-off was unplanned and uninvited by the St Kilda civic fathers: the publicly paraded promise of recreational sex.

St Kilda has one of the highest population densities of any city in Australia. Some 46 000 people inhabit just under eight square kilometres. There are few areas that are not at least partially residential. This has meant that the bulk of street prostitution has continued right in the heart of residential streets, intruding into the privacy of children at play. Resident groups that sprang up to protect themselves and their streets from gutter crawlers were sometimes remarkably successful. Self-help groups recorded the number plates of male clients and published them in the newspapers. They flashed torches in the eyes of drivers soliciting women, which often proved most effective. They threw rocks and buckets of water over street walkers and booby-trapped their gardens.

But unfortunately, street prostitution is like a water bed. When pushed down in one place, it bounces up in another. So what was one local street's victory became another's loss as it inherited the unwelcome trade.

The following history of prostitution comes from A. Longmire in *The Show Goes On: The History of St Kilda, Volume III, 1930–1983*, Hudson Publishing, Hawthorn, 1989, pp. 186ff.

Prostitution was not actually illegal in the past—the subject was unmentionable in polite circles, and unwritten laws about ladylike behaviour were believed to be sufficient to enforce morality. Some prostitutes were sent to convents to mend their immoral ways. Women could not be charged with soliciting under the Police Offences Act of 1928 unless the person solicited would cooperate and give evidence. Discussion of the presence of prostitutes in St Kilda was so taboo that complaints could not be dealt with in open council.

This did not stop the complaints, and in March 1932 a resident wrote this to the mayor:

Your park is littered with motor cars at night and goes right into the morning of the following day and disgraceful conduct is the order. Next morning when one goes to exercise his dog, it repeatedly picks up frog skins—you know what I mean.

During World War II Melburnians blamed St Kilda's infamous street prostitution for undermining the war effort. Too many young soldiers were seeking their 'rest and relaxation' in Fitzroy Street, St Kilda. In 1949, the first elections ever run anywhere in Australasia solely on the issue of prostitution were run in St Kilda. Extravagant electoral promises were made about expunging the shame and stain of prostitution from the city. Needless to say, despite so much posturing and strong words, the campaign made no dent in the commercial sex trade. Victorian morality and police action were no match for the sex industry. Nor were the Christian homes for 'young women at risk', nor the religion that was meant to inject some moral fibre into these women, able to stem the trade.

The issue would flare up from time to time, and St Kilda City Council took the risky step in 1978 of granting a permit to a massage parlour, effectively granting a trial run to the legalisation of prostitution. The parlour was humbly called the Something Incredible Saloon. It was allowed one masseur and offered striptease, twin massage, Japanese massage and suspender massage. Its advertisements featured a naked woman lying on a bed with a credit-card sign at her feet. Whatever its pretensions, it was a failed experiment and the council refused to issue another permit after twelve months.

The neighbouring council of Brighton demanded to be informed of any intention by its errant neighbour to license further brothels near its boundary. The pages of the local paper the *Southern Cross* became inflamed with moral and pecuniary rage. One former mayor wrote:

We are not concerned with the moral aspects of prostitution, but this type of activity must be somewhere that it does not affect decent people . . . Property values have declined by thirty per cent in some areas in the past two years and people are finding it impossible to sell their properties.

In reply, a member of the newly formed Prostitutes Action Group wrote this to the local paper:

Prostitutes get their reward. Not only financially, but by having good regular customers who won't use anybody but you. We are complimented on our skill and recommended to their friends . . . At least, I haven't sold my body for a lifetime merely to be lavished with wealth and to be made smart and 'respectable' . . . At least, I can set a time limit on my body—half an hour, an hour.

In 1979, the pressure to stamp out the steamy side of St Kilda became the focus of a major media hype. The Willesee program's television cameras exposed street walkers and drug deals with sensational footage of where drugs were obtainable. There was a barrage of articles that appeared in the metropolitan dailies using terms like 'streets of hell', 'devil's playground' and 'streets of death'. Derryn Hinch of Radio 3AW declared that he would be ashamed to be the Mayor of St Kilda. (I later said as mayor that I knew a number of ex-St Kilda mayors who would be ashamed to call themselves Derryn Hinch.)

This public shame and the outrage felt by St Kilda residents stung the council and the police into action. They launched a massive undercover police sting called Operation Zeta just before the State elections in May 1979 to clean up St Kilda once and for all. More than three thousand people were questioned and hundreds charged. Hotels were raided and police crawled through the area like flies at a barbecue. At the end of the operation, the detective superintendent in charge publicly and proudly announced: 'The riff-raff will not be allowed back in St Kilda.'

Well, the 'riff-raff' had news for the police. They well and truly bounced back! But more importantly, the conservative State Government held the seat of St Kilda by eighty-three votes and that gave it a one-seat majority to form a new government. The police timing was impeccable in granting the government electoral credit for 'cleaning up St Kilda'. It was not the first time that sex would be a determining factor in destroying or returning a government.

Who are these street prostitutes?

⤳

St Kilda was, in 1994, the one area in Melbourne that still had street prostitution. The Labor State Government had legalised brothels in 1985 and naively believed that this would obviate any need for street prostitution. Unhappily, there are just as many women in street prostitution in the mid 1990s as when it was illegal in 1985. In addition, many new workers have signed up for permanent employment in the legal brothels. The prospect of legal protection, regularised through normal taxation and medical supervision, appears to have attracted quite a new breed of sex worker. Some middle-class housewives have openly agreed with their husbands that they will pay off the second car or beach house through a few weekly shifts. Clever and attractive university students pay their way through college, and under-age private schoolgirls unhappy with the level of pocket money doled out by parents have been working to boost their expenses for partying and fashionable clothes.

Of course, the trap is that the lucrative earnings prove addictive in themselves. The lure of pay, often as high as $2000 per week, induces a lifestyle characterised by extravagance and luxury. Many who started to work at the soft end of the industry in topless massage or strip joints graduate to full prostitution, promising themselves that it will only be a short stint.

The knowledge that it is a limited career—until looks fade—and that every new client introduction carries the anxiety that this is possibly your uncle or neighbour introduces its own stress. Like just about everything else in life in these times, the bottom line is always money. Men may like to believe that sex workers are nymphomaniacs, and the smart sex worker may reinforce this fantasy to snare a booking. But the majority would still choose other work if it paid as lucratively as sex.

I have discovered a sure test to gauge how a sex worker feels about this 'socially acceptable, legal and safe profession'. When asked whether they would want their daughter to work in this 'industry', as it is euphemistically called, women are unequivocal: 'Absolutely not. I am working here to ensure that my daughter never has to!'

A survey found that most go into the industry for reasons of financial hardship, but more than a quarter said they would not change their profession if they could. One-third of women were married and over forty per cent had post-secondary qualifications. Seventy-nine per cent were Australian born and sixty-seven per cent had never injected drugs. At least one-third had dependent children.

The report's principal investigator said the survey dramatically challenged myths about Victoria's 1400 brothel workers. They were not trapped in this industry, or there against their will. On the contrary, they were responsible, normal women without sexually transmissible diseases (ninety-seven per cent reported always wearing condoms). Most were having their sexual health checked every four weeks, and less than one per cent said they had been coerced into this work. They exhibited mature independence and professionalism.

Street sex workers, by contrast, reveal a strikingly different social profile. They are almost all drug addicted and, therefore, when interviewed to work legally, are perfunctorily rejected on sight by the managers of brothels. They have considerably less sense of free will in the choice of this trade and certainly much less education. A high number have suffered incest, rape or some form of male abuse that has precipitated their drug addiction. This awful breach of trust from men translates into a determination that says, If someone could freely do that to me, then, by God, I'll make sure they pay for sex from now on. Whereas men tend to support their drug habits by either trafficking or burglaries, women more commonly supply their habit through prostitution.

Some of the street walkers, however, are not addicts, but single mothers who find the five- to eight-hour shifts at a legal brothel incompatible with their mothering responsibilities. For them, the prospect of a short stint on the street with the full financial rewards, because there are neither tax nor brothel management fees deducted, is worth the risk of rape and assault.

The murder of prostitutes on our streets

～

In February 1994, during my mayoral term, there was a brutal murder of a street worker. Samantha Misso was a mother of two young children from a close and a caring family in rural Victoria. She was a loving, friendly woman who worked on the streets casually when she needed some extra money. Her death was particularly chilling and obscene and was tragically followed by another death a couple of months later. The media reaction was instant—the combination of sex and death make for fantastic copy.

Her murderer is still unapprehended and may indeed be a multiple killer, as other murders of prostitutes show some similar traits. Naturally, this brings to mind the archetypal picture of the Yorkshire Ripper, and this collective memory triggers so much anger, fear and fantasy in every human heart. Anger was the dominant tone of some of the public commentators who pontificated smugly on the foolishness of street prostitution. Their comments seemed to suggest that Samantha Misso deserved all that violently befell her. They took the view that she would have been safe from murder if she were not engaged in an illegal and high-risk activity. Even some of the hardened professional sex workers dismissed these two victims as amateur part-timers who had moved in on the dangerous turf of the professionals.

This type of public response echoed the sentiments expressed a year earlier in the now infamous comments made by a County Court judge in a rape trial of a St Kilda prostitute. He authoritatively opined that a prostitute would not suffer nearly the same amount of personal trauma as an ordinary, decent woman would who was raped. Consequently, the judge imposed a lesser sentence on the convicted rapist of the prostitute.

The message was clear. Not all women are equal before the law. If you are morally bad, then it is less of a crime to rape you and, perhaps by extension, to murder you. The reaction to and debate on these murders educated the local community as to how cheapened some women's lives had become in our society.

I made strong and unequivocal public statements as the Mayor of St Kilda decrying the violence and calling for State Government measures to offer protection to street workers. Decriminalisation of street prostitution within some limited areas was, I reluctantly believed, worth a try. These demarcated and decriminalised streets could then include extra lighting, extra telephone boxes, some safe houses where prostitutes could flee, and a regular police drive-by to remind tourists that only sex, not other crimes, was decriminalised. Most significantly, decriminalisation would largely move street prostitution away from residential areas.

I realised that all this still might not save a Samantha Misso. Nothing could save a woman who got into the car of a social psychopath whose central locking system removed any possibility of escape. But at least it would mean that others might raise the alarm if a sex worker did not return, or the lighting might assist in noting the number plates of an offending car.

It was also my belief that decriminalisation might serve to encourage women workers to report vicious attacks to the police. Without this legislation they recoil from doing this because they are committing an offence in loitering for the purposes of prostitution in that area. I argued that when any group is treated as invisible by the law, they become an easy target for those whose psycho-sexual thrill consists of terrorising and assaulting them. Street prostitutes in St Kilda were suffering on average one rape a week and numerous assaults because their offenders relied on them not reporting such matters.

Naturally, these views raised the ire of the 'law and order' lobby. I was savaged by them and also by many in the wider Church. Others scoffed at such a simplistic suggestion as decriminalisation. They argued that if a burglar was committing a burglary, then why should any assault on the thief by the owner be reportable? Since these women are criminals, it was agreed, do not encourage them. If they want to avoid rape, murder or assault, then they should stop standing on dark street corners committing the crime of loitering. Simple. If they will not stop, then clearly they are beyond the reach of civilised society.

It was these strands of experience that helped focus my vision about the unfairness perpetuated by our laws. Why is it that the women street workers bear the brunt of social stigma and prosecution? They are charged by the police at a rate of ten women prostitutes for every one male client. Both female sex worker and male client are committing crimes, but historically the law was structured to blame the women. Perhaps this is not news to those educated in the legal biases of a male-dominated society, where it is assumed that men only stray because women mercilessly seduce them. But this patriarchal sexual illusion regrettably became an injustice framed in the law.

Australian State laws have weighted the evidentiary requirements to make it extraordinarily difficult to charge a man soliciting sex from a woman. Essentially, to get a conviction, a policewoman has to pose as a sex worker to extract evidence that a man has asked for sex in exchange for money. There is no crime until those words are uttered. Obviously it takes far fewer police, and therefore far fewer public resources, for a cruising police car to pick up a sex worker dressed in fishnet stockings and a miniskirt in a recognised redlight street. Her mere presence virtually establishes the elements of the charge of loitering for the purposes of prostitution. Strangely, a regular stream of charges for prostitution appears to satisfy public morality even though this is a victimless crime committed by two consenting adults.

The real offenders in terms of abuse of sex workers and the disturbance of residents are rarely the serious male clients.

Rather, they are the station-wagons and mini-buses full of half-tanked, aggressive voyeurs whose sole intent is to flash their car lights, toot their horns and shout degrading, offensive obscenities at women they regard as fair game for their chauvinistic bile. These are the ones who cause maximum anxiety and disturbance to the residents, and provoke the greatest sense of fear and repulsion in the women.

The serious clients, by contrast, furtively pull up, converse and collect the sex worker, then quietly and unobtrusively drive off. They avoid noise and attention like the plague. And working women develop a remarkable intuition for those who will be genuine clients and those who are the ugly mugs who come to abuse.

Priests and prostitutes

There is an old adage that goes like this: lawyers embezzle their clients' trust accounts, doctors end up addicted to prescription drugs, and ministers of religion have sexual affairs. The reasoning runs that there are particular occupational hazards in particular vocations. Perhaps it is equally true that people with a moral hairline fracture or besetting weakness are mysteriously and unconsciously drawn to callings that might expose those very weaknesses.

At any rate, there is a long history of those who are called to holy orders falling into an unholy estate. The projection by the congregation of God's righteousness onto God's representative, the clergyman, escalates the expectation of virtue to impossible heights. How many honest but fragile clergy have worn unfair and unrealistic expectations? How many have been startled to discover that their flock thought the call to ministry was accompanied by a corresponding loss of libido?

I guess for any clergy living in a place like St Kilda, the sexual possibilities present themselves more than they might in a safer, suburban context. I am equally sure, however, that temptation knows no geographic boundaries.

I well remember the warm Sunday summer night I walked the third of a kilometre back to our home after an evening service. A scantily clad woman approached me just as I drew near to our street corner. Now, in summer, most women walking around our sreets are scantily clad, so I did not immediately jump to any conclusions. She looked me in the eye and asked if I was interested in her services, or something to that effect. Given the fact that we were right outside a large block of flats that backed onto my home, I decided to ask a few questions. My wife Merridie had suspected for a few weeks that there were some strange activities happening over the fence.

After giving a quick quote of the menu and prices, the woman then indicated that her 'place' was indeed within the block of flats right behind where she stood. Other women were also plying the trade within a few yards of us. I was honestly untempted by the wares she had on offer, especially when her massive pimp started swaggering towards us. But I did walk home with determination to explore the legality of what was obviously an unregistered brothel. The flats in question housed a number of longer-term elderly residents that I knew, including one of our church's deacons. A few telephone conversations later saw the Vice and Gaming Squad come and close the brothel down. But I knew this was only shifting it into someone else's backyard.

Andrew Dutney, an Australian Uniting Church Minister in his book *Food, Sex and Death: A Personal Account of Christianity*, has pointed out that there has been an awkward and convoluted relationship between the clergy and sex:

> And marriage, endorsed and ordered by the church, was understood by the church as a concession to human frailty and a remedy for sin . . . Lay marriage was therefore given over to procreation, and thus to human weakness and the perpetuation of original sin. Clerical marriage was given over to celibacy, and thus to spiritual power and holiness.

He further notes:

> Whether it was based on the Hebrew idea of the semen as defiling or on the Greco-Roman idea of orgasm as enfeebling, there was a suspicion by the second century which developed into an insistence by the fourth century that sex and ministry did not mix. Sexual activity, even within marriage, was considered to compromise the minister's ability to fulfil the duties of a holy office.

Naturally, this rigid and debilitating worldview soon saw rigid and debilitating roles foisted onto men and women. Holy ministries were soon an exclusively male domain, and worldliness, weakness and sin were increasingly associated with women, from whom these holy men were to be kept.

The debasement of sex and women had begun with the need to provide a theological explanation for the universality of sin. Its universality was most logically explained by the sex act. Since all humans were conceived through intercourse, it must be the sex act that infected them all with original sin. Augustine had hinted at this and Aquinas later settled the question. He taught that, indeed, it was the sex act that was the beginning point of transmission of our universal sinful rebellion from God. Sex, which had originally been declared good and a gift of God in the Genesis account of creation, was now impugned by the Church theologians as the conveyor of the spiritual virus (sin) that leads to the spiritual death of all humans.

Sex and sin have long been the dual enemies of the 'man of God'. Being a Baptist minister and a mayor and making pronouncements on a murdered prostitute led some sectors of the press to believe that I might just add the ideal missing ingredient in the story—a clerical wowserism that judgmentally declared the victim's sinfulness to have been duly punished. Was not the wages of sin death, as the old book said?

In this, they were sorely disappointed. To the shock of many whose historical memory hungered for some time-worn stereotypical clergy response, I thoroughly confused the punters, not to mention the faithful. I was asked in an interview for the Melbourne *Age* if I envied the people I worked with, such as prostitutes. I replied that I did:

> There is no mask, because there is simply no pretension to them whatsoever. That raw honesty I really do envy. That's what Jesus meant when he talked about the prostitutes entering the kingdom before the righteous. In the kingdom of life, it's that honesty, it's that vulnerability, that need for grace that is so important.

Jesus, friend of prostitutes

As a follower of Jesus of Nazareth, I had reason to reflect deeply on his friendship with those beyond the reach of civilised religious society: the publicans, prostitutes and despised tax collectors. The religious establishment of Jesus' time believed that if every Jew could obey the law for just a 24-hour period, then the Messiah would return, liberating Israel and instituting the reign of God on earth.

The ones thwarting this exciting prospect in the eyes of the doctors of the Religious Establishment were the very people Jesus included as his special friends. He was dignifying their immorality by being seen at their parties. His open company became a religious scandal, as he was holding back the righteous tide of history and the return of the Messiah. Little wonder these leaders started to plot his death. In their eyes, and by their criteria, Jesus was an unspeakable blasphemer.

Something of this gospel scandal was illuminated at a worship service at the House of Hope, a street-front community in St Kilda, in early 1994. The biblical text was the story of Jesus enjoying hospitality at the home of Simon the Pharisee. At the height of the feast, a woman of ill repute gatecrashed the party. She anointed Jesus' head with oil and wiped his feet with her hair. Stunned by this, the guests present and Simon the host expressed shock that Jesus' judgment was so bad that he, a religious teacher, had allowed himself to receive physical care from such a tainted woman. One could hear the audible gasps of shock from the righteous ones.

After the reading of this story, one of the congregation called 'Gay', herself a street worker in St Kilda, decided to comment. She was amazed at the courage of the biblical woman who risked total rejection. Gay said she had seen the parties on St Kilda Hill where BMWs pulled up outside Victorian mansions, letting out beautiful people dressed in extravagant clothes. They danced and partied in lavish style. She knew how dreadfully impossible it was for her to even contemplate gatecrashing because of the disgust that her presence would evoke. Her contribution to the discussion in the worship service on this biblical passage was what an incredible person Jesus must be to command such courage from a woman like her. What sort of love and acceptance did he offer that this woman in the Bible should risk social suicide and total rejection?

Gay's insight was profound and left all those in the worship service with a fresh way of seeing the meaning of the story. She understood the text in its rawest, most direct form because she had put herself into the story. She was closer to the power of its liberation and truth than any of us from more respectable backgrounds.

Local government: friend of prostitutes?

In all of this hype and publicity, the long-suffering residents of St Kilda's more notorious streets were organising themselves. They had discussions with the Prostitutes Collective of Victoria and agreed to support decriminalisation. Long before this, they had come to accept that the council was incapable of helping them. We at the City Hall only had blunt remedies like putting in one-way traffic flows and roundabouts to shape the speed and direction of the gutter crawlers. Engineering solutions were always going to prove utterly inadequate to solve entrenched social problems.

The residents had developed a mature and radically sophisticated approach. They had isolated the precise problem and named it as essentially neither the prostitutes nor their clients. They were emphatic that their home-and-hearth peace was being disturbed by the aggressive tourist traffic, not the sex workers. For a group of residents to pinpoint the voyeurs and not simply blame the sex workers was a quantum leap.

The campaign for decriminalisation flexed some real political muscle with the creation of a lobby group comprising residents, local council, the Prostitutes Collective and the Salvation Army. Melbourne, known as the city of caution and conservatism, was being confronted with articulate spokespersons from a diverse political and social base. They pointedly asked why the government looked the other way to avoid seeing the assault and abuse of women on its streets. Was it not utterly hypocritical to leave some sex workers bereft of any real protection, given that Victoria was one of the few States in Australia that had legalised brothels?

All agreed on one thing: the naming of a non-residential, probably industrial street area—complemented with good lighting, visibility and no schools, churches or homes nearby—was the best solution. Decriminalistion merely extended the accepted policy of regulation of the industry. A century of moral ranting against the evil, and costly and useless police campaigns were a monumental failure. Worse still, they had significantly intensified the publicity and misery suffered by both residents and sex workers.

The message seemed clear. This was essentially not a moral issue, as moral qualms had not prevented the legalisation of brothels. This was a power issue. There were no votes in protecting the poorest and most vulnerable women. Nor were there votes in removing prostitution from residential streets. St Kilda residents would again be treated as if they were inhabitants of another planet. The government and the police made unabashed admissions that further crackdowns and repression of street prostitution would fail.

But despite a sensitive and intelligent campaign, the

political stomach to embrace laws that permitted prostitution in designated areas and under clear controls, as in New South Wales, was simply not there. Safety was secondary to political opportunism. Again, those completely unaffected by the nightmare of this reality made their political decisions from afar.

The law: friend of prostitutes?

What is the aim of the law in prosecuting sex workers and their clients? I have represented hundreds of women in court. The only two men on whose behalf I appeared, who had been entrapped in the periodic police crackdowns, have not been deterred. Policewomen will tell you how demoralising it is to stand on a dark street corner playing the honey-pot prostitute, begging for convictions in beauty's disguise. What is the point? Men charged with soliciting sometimes freak at the possibility that their wife and friends will find out through publicity given to a court conviction. But very few are charged and there is no serious deterrence.

The court and its administration will wearily apply the appropriate punishment, recognising its complete futility to deter, rehabilitate or punish. The court fines imposed can only be paid by more prostitution. The law is no longer justified in religious or moral terms. That undergirding for any prosecution has long since slipped. The Victorian parliament has declared that, since no-one gets hurt in consensual private agreements, the exchanging of sex for money between adults is perfectly legal as long as it is in a registered brothel. Foolishly, the criminal law is employed against street workers to regulate commercial trade and its acceptable location. Is that its proper role?

The married man: friend of prostitutes?

⤙

It comes as somewhat shattering news to discover that by far the majority of male clients of women of the night are married men. They visit brothels for a vast array of reasons. And, surprisingly, they are not always the obvious ones whom one would perhaps expect to be giving expression to their screaming hormones. Loneliness, vulnerability and longing for an acceptance of male angst and fragility are all at play. The prospect of intimate talk with detachment and objectivity and without ongoing emotional engagement—because this is 'sex, not love'—often suits both client and sex worker. The sex worker who is mature and sufficiently intelligent to offer an understanding ear finds anguished hearts pouring out their sense of aloneness in marriage. With the shrinking role of the Church, and particularly the loss of the anonymity which the confessional box provided, the anonymity of a listening ear in the brothel may be picking up the slack.

But what psychology is at play in men whose nocturnal cravings stimulate the demand for commercial street sex? What is the interior life of men who choose the dark streets and gutter crawling and disdain the Prussian orderliness of a safe, legal brothel? Certainly, there is the element of male control that is lost in a brothel. To enter a brothel and be seen by others is an admission of need and pity. It is to be seen for who you are in all your bravado and folly and to start on equal footing with the sex worker. The thrill for some men is located in their need for control, so they seek an environment where they project their fantasies onto a woman. The demystification of this feverish fantasy has already begun in a brothel because both prostitute and client can observe each other and form their own conclusion. The sex worker might even turn the view among the street workers: that some police were often after 'freebie sex' and were not to be trusted. My judgments of Julie dissolved when she told me how she had been raped at fifteen by one of the many different men who passed through her mother's life and home. She felt so 'dirty' that she decided she would never let any man do that to her again. She would at least make them pay! I understand how in a tragically coherent way she was taking power back over her life. Who was I to judge?

Her tour ended with our arrival at the meal program. Unannounced, she commanded silence by telling everyone, including those serving, to shut up because she wanted to introduce her lawyer, who was the best legal eagle in town. I politely waved to the many street people gathering for lunch and lined up and got my dinner. When more people drifted in, Julie was clearly perturbed that they had missed the benefit of her announcement, so she got on her feet again to reintroduce me. I felt acutely stiff and self-conscious in my formal court suit and wondered whether I should hand out my business cards, make a speech or just disappear. From a distant table, someone commented in a loud voice: 'God, things must be bad if lawyers have to eat here.'

Lunching with prostitutes was one way to start my ministry. It probably isn't the way most Baptist ministers start out. As I found myself becoming aware of my new surrounds and the common threads running through the various subcultures, I discovered that the world of prostitution, one of those cultures, went on twenty-four hours a day. It is all so visible.

I remember driving along in the van one day with a clutch of children on board when our seven-year-old daughter Claire asked my wife Merridie what a lady was doing leaning against a post. In a flash, her nine-year-old friend replied that the lady tables by deciding she will not take a booking with the client because he is ugly or drunk. That prospect is terrifying to a male.

But in a car travelling on a dark street, a man retains both personal anonymity and the personal power to roar off totally unsighted by others. The considerable advantage of circling a number of times, flashing one's headlights onto full beam and sensually savouring the female talent reminds men of their strength. It is an intoxicating lure to the emotionally impotent male to have women act like sexual bait. The humiliation of male power through ever-advancing feminism is momentarily turned back.

Here, the male as hunter, warrior and gatherer still reigns unchallenged. The warrior aspect is fundamental to the thrill. True warriors risk considerable danger, which serves to heighten the testosterone thrill. It is the men in blue uniform and sometimes in unmarked police cars who are the danger. They pose the threat of loss of reputation and even loss of freedom. But this merely nourishes the sexual adrenaline.

This truly is still a male predator's world. What a contrast to the grey contemporary world where bourgeois married men uniformly dressed in suits inhabit spiritless offices and call themselves managers. In what we regard as this politically correct, feminist-shaped world, such many believe they are being tamely re-educated to be sensitive, New Age guys who risk death from self-flagellation.

Sexuality and spirituality

⁓

What are we really struggling with in this moral extremity? Clearly, the need to offer some safety to those women who play the street game is paramount. Any ethical system (Christian or humanist) must balance competing considerations. Preserving public morality and sensibilities are to be given weight in a civilised society. But when they have largely been ditched through the parliament's embrace of legalised prostitution, we must ask whose interests are being served by a law that places some drug-affected, unemployable women way beyond any real protection. Is that not pandering to the brooding, primeval instincts of men who should be made responsible for their personal sexual pursuits by having to encounter women in well-lit streets and not be allowed to stalk in dark residential alleys?

Another force unleashed is the sheer compulsive drive of sexuality. Our world is thoroughly secularised. One hallmark of secularity is the 'freeing' of sexuality from any religious framework and from any moral inhibition or taboo. Whilst this may have had its advent with Sigmund Freud, he would probably express shock at the candid public level of sexual discourse and our unblushing frankness about promiscuity.

I remember counselling one attractive eighteen-year-old woman living in St Kilda who wanted help with her depression. The cause of her blues was the timeless 'love gone wrong' scenario. Her boyfriend had left and she wanted him back. When I probed the reasons for his flight, she told me it was a trifling matter. I persisted by pressing for a little more detail. She casually said he had come back to their flat and found her in bed with another man. She found it virtually incomprehensible that he would treat this 'trifling misdemeanour' as serious enough grounds to leave.

Whilst this young woman may seem badly out of touch, she certainly represents a whole generation that finds it easier to fake love by making love rather than honouring sexual intimacy as the treasured expression of a fundamental emotional and spiritual commitment between a man and a woman. Many people, paradoxically, find it easier to take their clothes off and explore each other's bodies than to take their masks off and admit their fear of commitment and rejection.

Sadly, the buying of sex is perhaps the paradigm of intimacy in a culture that commodifies life. Prostitution may have become the most honest barometer of the worth of sex in a culture that can only value life in economic language. Is this not the loss of sexuality right in the midst of a sex-saturated culture that presses its face into every ad and TV program we watch?

This loss was brilliantly named in the film *Last Tango in Paris*. A man and a woman have an abandoned, erotic, 24-hour orgy. But passion turns to pathology and the hollow emptiness of the experience breaks in with the woman finally killing her lover in an attempt to escape. She stands over his corpse with tears streaming down her face, repeatedly saying, 'I don't even know who he is. I never even knew his name.'

I have often wondered at the inordinate advertising resource that the hunger for sex permits. When we moved into our first home in St Kilda, mail would keep arriving for the previous owner who had lived there until his death. We kept returning it to sender, but a persistent video/magazine outlet kept us on their mailing list. Eventually, one of our young children opened the curious brown envelope. It was from a pornography mail-order company based in Canberra and was full of the perverse, fleshy delights available through them. It is a massive industry built on lust. We only shook off their persistence when Merridie wrote in large red print on yet another brown envelope that arrived: 'The old bugger's been dead for seven years and the stuff you've fed him probably hasn't helped where he's ended up!' It seemed to do the trick.

The hunger for sex is a misplaced hunger for spirituality. That may come as a surprise to many. Sex and God appear to be unrelated, but I suspect that they are constantly confused. Sexuality and spirituality are two sides of the same coin. They both aim at providing union, oneness and intimacy. Vulnerability as symbolised in physical or spiritual nakedness is a cry for love and acceptance. Wholeness is experienced by fragmented, alienated parts being melded together. The words of the Hebrew Scriptures so often quoted at a wedding service bring this wholeness alive: 'For this reason shall a man leave his mother and father and cling to his wife and the two shall become one.' Sex by itself is a totally inadequate substitute for the intimacy we crave as spiritual beings.

The obsessional search for orgasm promoted by *Cleo* and *Playboy* magazines, among others, takes on more weighty dimensions than just sexual technique. Pulling and pressing the right tabs of flesh are a much inferior way to inflame the erotic passions than the lost romantic arts of poetry, song and spiritual celebration. But so many seriously study the mechanics of sex in the forlorn hope of finding some self-identity—even finding God.

The moment of orgasm for many is the closest thing they ever feel to a spiritual experience. In that moment, they feel loved and alive; they are somebody. However, it passes and the letdown of loneliness descends like the sinking of the last glow of a sunset. In the dark place lies an empty soul.

A safe place for sex—or the death of sex?

﹏

The search for God turns to ashes when it is mistakenly identified as a search for sex. It becomes a disorientating reversal of the whole meaning order. Knowing our identity and our spiritual home is the foundation upon which a healthy sex life is based. When sex is substituted as the foundation, instead of a relationship with God, we end up projecting destructive expectations onto our partners which they can never fulfil. To know a safe and welcoming place in sex, we have to first know that safe place within ourselves and within our universe. Spiritual security breeds greater sexual joy.

The commitment of marriage has traditionally been understood as that safe place. It is where one's sexual performance is not the cement for the relationship. Rather, marriage provides a free and secure relational space to take risks, laugh and learn together, even while behaving as fumbling, faltering sexual amateurs. It is one of the last places of refuge in life where one is not primarily judged by performance. In fact, within the base commitment that marriage symbolises, the freedom is given for an exciting mutual adventure of discovery and experimentation. The security of marriage permits one to fail without the chronic anxiety that performance is everything and that failure will result in automatic rejection. Our partner is committed for 'better or worse' and this is a radically different contract to the tyranny of those that require a performance review every twelve months.

Julie, my first legal client, had taught me about the longing for acceptance and a safe place. Her acceptance of me and introduction to her world's dangers and threats had touched me. She was not just a prostitute. That term mercilessly categorises and unfairly defines her whole being, as if being someone's mother and someone's daughter is irrelevant. Julie was a person first and foremost. Julie still is, as far as I know. Julie is a woman of worth—no matter where life's circumstances have taken her.

Julie as a woman exuded a hospitable, kindly persona that included her sexuality. But celibate and single people also exude a sexuality that is part of their whole character. This richer notion of sexuality as part of personality frees us to enjoy others' sexuality without seeking to be sexual partners or sexual conquerors. This marvellously liberates us all from a narrow performance-oriented world that strives to measure our sexuality in orgasmic quantities or, as with prostitution, in monetary terms.

Prostitution, as sex for money, is not a pressing or real social problem for most of us. But its public profile in social and political debate may have symbolically elevated it to the status of the yardstick by which we quantify sexual need and its service satisfaction. A society that can clinically regulate this 'service provision' whilst still cherishing its moral hypocrisy and storing up its righteous rage to dump periodically on street prostitutes is one that risks the very death of sex.

Sex as a gift freely, lovingly and relationally offered grants true security and safety. Such sex within a truly safe place of a committed relationship (which historically we recognise as the institution of marriage) is an extraordinary gift of creativity to enrich human existence. It is the antithesis of the social and legal humbug, epitomised in the prostitution laws, that immortalise a commercialisation of sex.

Charting my course

People often ask me how I ended up simultaneously a lawyer, a minister of a church, and a city councillor, a position which led to my being Mayor of St Kilda. I sometimes ask myself the same question. My getting to St Kilda is populated with influences, experiences and people. All of them deserve a mention to make some sense of what has unfolded.

I grew up in leafy Blackburn, a great place to be a kid in the 1960s. Saturdays were spent wandering far and wide, exploring the parks and riding our bikes without a thought of stranger danger or the perils that beset children's play today. Blackburn is a homely middle-class suburb some eighteen kilometres east of Melbourne, in a general area which is sometimes referred to as the Bible belt.

My parents settled in a new estate on former fecund orchard groves and, nearly half a century on, they are still in the same house. In these days of transience, it is satisfying and centring to watch one's children play with some of the same toys one played with in the same family home. Life consisted of backyard football and cricket, a lively and loving family, sport at school and church on Sundays. I knew and loved all four of my grandparents, who lived in other suburbs of Melbourne.

Mum was a full-time secondary teacher and later an educational psychologist. She had beaten the medical odds, for doctors had told her that the rheumatic fever that had nearly claimed her life in her early teens meant she would never be able to have children. In fact she produced three healthy children: myself, my brother Peter, and our sister Janet, in that order. Dad taught at Carey Baptist Grammar for thirty-three years, his only permanent teaching position. His chance to become a teacher came under the generous government terms for soldiers returned from World War II which enabled them to undertake university courses.

My parents represented that peculiar pragmatism and sectarianism which had characterised Australian religion and politics for generations past. Dad was baptised Catholic and was from a working-class, Labor-voting family on his mother's side that was as Irish as Paddy's pig. But the family were lapsed Catholics and did not attend any church. Mum was from Scottish–English parents who were solid Presbyterians, fervent believers in the Prime Minister, Mr Menzies, and strong supporters of the Liberal Party. The Methodists came to claim my father's religious allegiance because, to play in their local cricket team, one had to attend their church at least once a month. He was around the age of nineteen when he started this association and it led to his deep conversion to an evangelical faith in Christ.

My parents' backgrounds (as was the case with many marriages of that era) brought together two very strong and opposing forces in Australia.

Irish Catholics and Presbyterians had clashed bitterly in full sectarian rage over issues like loyalty to the British Crown from almost the beginning of white settlement in Australia, and later, in World War I, over conscription. Catholics initally were unwelcome and unwanted in the Liberal Party when it was formed in 1949.

My parents' wedding day in 1953 in the Murrumbeena Presbyterian Church had to be on the Saturday morning, as Dad's side needed to get away to watch the football in the afternoon (much to the horror of my mother's family). Dad's brother, a practising Catholic, came to the wedding but stood outside the church, as there was no dispensation to enter a Protestant church in those sectarian times.

After settling in Blackburn, my parents chose to attend neither the Presbyterian nor the Methodist churches, but the Baptist, which was marginally closer to home. Perhaps it was a happy compromise. Distance was at any rate an important non-religious consideration, as they were not to own their first car, an FJ Holden, for another seven years. Certainly it meant that they were part of a small group that met together and from which a very large and influential church was to grow.

I attended Blackburn Baptist Church with my family, and I appreciate the fact that it was neither fundamentalist nor liberal. It gave me an appreciation of the Christian faith and the need for it to be relevant in today's world. I credit my two pastors, the Reverend David Griffiths and the Reverend Rowland Croucher, with informing my developing faith in positive and creative ways in that church. Family and Church functions were the cornerstones in a white Anglo-Saxon world, where loyalty to the Queen and producing progeny that would later be termed the baby boomers characterised the international and local horizons. It was a socially, racially and religiously homogeneous and stable world. We met with other families over Sunday roast dinners, where lively discussions would be the order of the day. Television brought us my favourite clowns, Zig and Zag, and Mr Menzies' voice reassured us over the radio that all was well in the world, especially the British Commonwealth, which we identified by the colour crimson in our school atlases. I remember that, in my secure family and Sunday school world, even as a child of six I consciously accepted what was explained to me as 'Jesus knocking on my heart's door'. I was always an eager child and anything that offered new possibilities I grasped with excitement.

My childlike faith was shaped in an environment of caring adults, including a few who took a special interest in me; this is in contrast to stories that were told of me tearing up Sunday school classes. At a conference years later a woman let me know I had given her great encouragement for her own children. She remembered me as the biggest ratbag in church and Sunday school, and yet I had turned out okay. Despite this I did however, accrue a good knowledge of the Bible, but most importantly its stories which fired my imagination and imparted a deeply personal faith, modelled on my parents' lives.

My early teenage years were fraught with typical pubescent anxieties. I was self-conscious when it came to girls, and I slowly and painfully realised I was not going to achieve my heart-felt ambition to be an AFL footballer or an Australian cricketer. I suffered a knee injury in my early teens and then was hospitalised with glandular fever in Year 11, which did not help my sporting prowess or my general confidence. Nor did a fairly heavy dose of acne. However, the strong roots of friendship and support through my church did enable my faith to develop.

It was at Carey Grammar that I undertook my secondary education. I loved school, I loved sport, and I loved studying history and politics in particular. Dad taught both of them and kept both Peter and me on our toes as we discussed and argued over current affairs. Sometimes we went for each other like a pair of Queensland blue heelers, as our sport and debates were pretty competitive. Neither of us could help noticing that Dad read the daily newspapers from cover to cover—my kids think I've learnt that trait well. He also taught us boys to passionately support the Essendon football club. We learnt this through regular Saturday afternoon sorties out to Windy Hill. It was our passionate secret men's business.

In my later years at school I tried to integrate my Christian faith into my life and to influence my peers. I probably did more damage than good. I also got involved in a few organisations that did evangelism on the beaches over the summer. This taught me skills in public speaking, thinking quickly on my feet, and coping with hostile responses. All have been extremely useful to me as a lawyer and a pastor. I especially note the influence of Robert Coyle, a tireless evangelist and trainer of young people. Rob befriended me and provided me with many opportunities in leadership and preaching. John Smith, the founder of God's Squad and other Christian ministries in Melbourne, was also a mentor to me in many ways. His passionate preaching and identification with the marginal groups in society inspired and challenged me.

In my last year at school, I attended a leadership training week for young Christians. John Smith was one of the speakers. It was there I saw a shy girl sitting in front of me and had an intuitive feeling she would one day be my wife. I met her later and found out that she was the only sister of five elder brothers from a well-known Baptist family. She says her first impression of me was that I was a loud-mouthed clown dominating the volleyball court. This was Merridie Kitchen.

She and I soon became good friends, and after seven on-again, off-again years of courtship, we enshrined our feelings in our marriage vows on 12 May 1979. This was despite my father's threats that there would be no wedding present from him if I married before thirty. He hadn't married until he was over thirty and, as a child of the Great Depression, believed in a job and a home deposit before romance transformed into commitment. We somehow surmounted that hurdle, and even scored a piano as a present from Mum and Dad. Merridie shared with me a strong conviction that God was central to what was worthwhile in life. We also found that our interests and senses of humour were extremely well-matched.

University in between times
⌁

The dream of my youth was to end up being a full-time evangelist, an old-style preacher who travelled the land. To that extent, I could not decide what to do when I left school. University dawned and doing a law degree seemed logical, but at seventeen it was all a bit unfocussed.

University in the mid-1970s was a feeling of having missed the mainstage performance. The idealism, protest and action of the 1960s had ebbed and a new society based on sharing, love and peace had failed to show up. In fact, it had been betrayed by the rip-off merchants and LSD peddlers of Haight Ashbury. The moral rage that had unified a generation against the war in Vietnam had been dissipated with Whitlam pulling all the Aussie troops out. We were left with the slogans 'Make love and not war' and 'Don't trust anyone over thirty', but no constructive historical project. The Left never found an equivalent cause to Vietnam in the 1970s, and many students felt they were living off former radical stories.

University was great for socialising, personal growth, and even some educational pursuits. The latter were strictly optional. We knew that less than five per cent of the population received tertiary training and, as the elite, there would be jobs whatever our grades. How different our experience was to the anxiety and pressure of today where secondary students have to do brilliantly to get into law and then have to do brilliantly at law school and university to land a legal job. I am amazed to see, when I go back on to campuses to speak, students in the cafeteria bent over their books studying in their lunchbreaks. That was definitely non-kosher in my time.

Prime Minister Whitlam had abolished tertiary fees and opened up diplomatic relations with China; great hopes rested on his redefinition of Australian life. Stories of fantastic jobs in the dramatically expanded federal public service filtered back to university. His government had majestic plans of one-stop shops to solve every imaginable human problem, a place in the Australian sun for marginalised groups like artists, women, Aborigines and migrants, and an enlarged role for the public sector. All this promised an Australian society forever changed.

But others, like my family and friends in Blackburn, feared and distrusted any such socialist future. At the historic 1972 'It's Time' election that brought in a federal Labor government for the first time in twenty-three years, Peter and I were paid by the Liberals to hand out 'How to Vote' cards for a Liberal candidate without any electoral prospects in a staunch northern metropolitan Labor seat. It was our political blooding and we were on the wrong side of the Australian people's will and history.

At university I spent my time actively involved in the Evangelical Union, a group of two hundred students that ran Christian lectures and studied the Bible and its application to life. I became the president of this group and my brother Peter became the first political candidate it went out to publicly support. It was the beginning for me of a convergence between the twin loves of my life—religion and politics. I was developing a growing realisation that the two are inseparable.

I was also running a weekly home group for my church, to which twenty or more young people would come. We would look at the Bible together and seek to support each other in prayer.

It was in this group that one night in 1975 I met a 'mature-age' (all of twenty-seven) hippie called Bill Hallam, who had a huge beard and hair down to his seat. He had left Australia in the late sixties to follow the hippie trail through Asia and into India, where he studied for years in a Hindu ashram. On the way, his search for truth had led him to a strong Christian faith through a communal group called Dilaram House, which had set up refuges along the hippie trail. He and I became close friends and talked wildly of founding an inner-city community that took faith and justice seriously. Some important seeds for the future were planted in me by our long and impassioned conversations. Some years later, after we had both spent time in Europe, Bill was to become my co-worker in St Kilda.

Another experience that influenced the direction life began to take for me was a stint I did as a youth pastor at Oakleigh Baptist Church. I began it in 1978 whilst doing my Diploma of Education at Monash University and finishing my term as the president of the Evangelical Union. It meant leaving Black-burn Baptist and becoming involved in a different sort of church. Oakleigh was lower-middle class and had quite a different ethos. I had to quickly simplify my content and make it more practical. I enjoyed the earthy hospitality of the people of Oakleigh and, with Merridie's help, we built up a team around us that eventually led a home group of over sixty young adults.

Over the next two years I began to find myself feeling it was not all holding together and I was becoming increasingly unsure what church was all about. Merridie and I were married by this stage and both working full-time. The youth group was burgeoning, but we knew we needed further training and wider input to help us answer some of the questions that were emerging from our experience. A young man in the group committed suicide after bouts of severe depression, and a family went through enormous upheaval around their son's homosexuality. Our theology and experience proved too limited to deal with the complexity of these pastoral issues we were facing.

On top of that, two years of doing mainly family law in a suburban firm found me feeling restless about working at the crisis end of family life, rather than at the preventive end. The practice of law had become a bit disillusioning, as it seemed to me to be more about budgets and less about justice. I acknowledged to myself a desire to undertake some serious theological study and to look at addressing these complexities in the years to come.

Life in Switzerland

—

At the very end of 1980, Merridie and I left Australia to pursue some years of study at a Baptist seminary in Rueschlikon, some

ten kilometres from Zurich, Switzerland. We arrived in a snow-
storm, straight out of a baking Australian summer.

It was stepping out into the unknown in more ways than
one. Neither of us had travelled overseas before. And people
we knew had mixed responses to the notion of our studying
at Rueschlikon. Some feared we would lose our faith altogether
under the influence of liberal theology. But we both knew we
had to get away and that this offered us both a unique opportunity to study and to grow without all the trappings of home
bearing down upon us.

The Baptist Seminary at Rueschlikon was an international
institution that trained men and women from around the world
to be Baptist ministers and theologians. In 1995 it was relocated
to Prague. In our time the student body numbered around
seventy and it was a global smorgasbord, drawing people from
every continent. Students were thrown together in an English-
speaking island. Most did not speak German and knew no-one
else outside the seminary. For some of our time there we were
the only Australians. The East European students had been
forced to leave their wives and children behind as insurance
to their communist governments that they would not defect.
Others from Africa or Asia simply could not afford to bring
them. Loneliness and cultural isolation were as keenly felt as
the lingering, long, snow-bound winters.

We set up our home in a bedsit apartment in a block about
a hundred metres from the magnificent ivy-covered double-
storeyed mansion which was the centre of the seminary. It was
set on a hill, with glorious views of the length and breadth of
Lake Zurich. To the east were glimpses of the medieval city
of Zurich, and to the north, in the distance, a clear day would
reveal towering scenic alps that were snow-capped all year
round. Directly across the lake nestled the village of Kustnacht

and the lakeside home of the famous Swiss psychiatrist Carl Jung. I was later to take some courses at the institute there that bears his name.

Being in Switzerland we became a mecca for many travelling Aussies. In our first three months we entertained at least thirty friends or friends of friends. Our cramped accommodation meant our hospitality was frequently a talking point, especially when people arrived with next to no warning and we all bunked in together. This just was not the Swiss way of doing things.

Beyond the college gates was a country that needed no marketing. It was a tourist's dream. Its natural features of valleys and peaks were as pretty and perfect as depicted on many a chocolate-box cover. But socially Switzerland was unbending in its work ethic and decidedly unwelcoming to foreigners. The Swiss Germans seemed to be so focussed on work that they neglected hospitality and friendship. All the roads were cleared of snow before dawn. Litter and uncleanliness were akin to blasphemy against the Holy Ghost. The buses and trains all ran perfectly on time, but the milk of human kindness was often strikingly absent.

I remember stepping onto a suburban bus bound for Zurich and holding the door open whilst Merridie, who was heavily pregnant with our first child, walked awkwardly up to the bus some metres behind me. The bus had only a few people on it and I explained in my best German that my wife was pregnant. The driver would not look at me and loudly shouted his annoyance and tried to shut the doors and take off. The passengers glowered menacingly at this foreigner who threatened to plunge their trip into a twenty-second delay. As I held my ground in the door frame, breaking the automatic closing device to let Merridie on, I felt like a Baader-Meinhof terrorist.

Swiss people in the German canton where we lived

expected submissive social conformity from their offspring to the authoritarian wisdom of their elders. But by the time we arrived in the country, this type of authoritarian decency and order was starting to be challenged. We made our first trip into Zurich in early January 1981, only to be confronted by Swiss youth rioting and pelting the police with rocks. Tear gas was fired back and violent arrests followed. When we enquired about this phenomenon, we discovered that fourteen years after student unrest had provoked uprisings in France and Germany, the protest movement had reached Switzerland. Swiss youth had finally had enough of parental and cultural repression and in the summer of 1980 had marched naked through the main streets of Zurich, causing the gnomes in the grand banking houses to blush and turn their heads.

The Swiss were dumbfounded at this challenge to the given order. They had been spared the passion and madness of the sixties only for it to erupt now. In their minds there was only one explanation. This was German communist-inspired subversion of their youth, who would never dream of such insubordination left to themselves. None of them considered that it might track back to suffocatingly tight control—blame lay squarely at the feet of the rabble-rousing Germans.

Swiss conservatism is indicated in the failure of Switzerland to join the United Nations—it is thought to be a left-wing front. Another indication is that women were only granted the national vote in 1967. We visited the canton of Appenzeller, where women still did not have the cantonal vote in 1983. When I asked some of the women shopkeepers how they felt about this extraordinary limitation on their political liberty, they smiled and explained, as if to a slow child, that they fully trusted their menfolk's ability to make the right laws. Gender-restricted democracy was conducted in the canton's main square by the raising of hands. It was good for business to have tourists like us coming to look at their quaint process of law-making.

Special laws ensured that *Ausländern*, or foreigners, did not receive full civil or political rights. Their presence was barely tolerated and they were made to feel their illegitimacy. I doubt that this was officially sanctioned other than in a general wariness about being flooded by migrants. All Swiss men between the ages of eighteen and fifty did two weeks' unpaid military training. Conscientious objection was openly ridiculed and virtually unknown. This was a country that took nothing for granted and maintained a vigilance that suspected all others and trusted no-one else in the world.

Many of the laws dated back to the Reformation when some cantons became Protestant. One of our professors was washing his car one Sunday when the cantonal police pulled up to book him for breaking the sabbath law. The neighbour who had reported him had done so not because he was religious, but because it was a four-centuries-old law. The religious reason and substance had completely disappeared in secular Switzerland, but the Swiss insisted that the shell of the law still be enforced.

During our years in Switzerland, our first child was born. This was, of course, a momentous and emotional moment. We had not asked to know the gender of the baby, so it was disappointing to be told by our Swiss gynaecologist while he took an ultrasound that it was a boy and to have medical technology seem to remove the mystery for us. We carefully chose the boy's name and excitedly prepared an announcement sheet to send back home to relatives and friends. We took the headline, 'It's a boy!', off an English paper we had from Prince William's birth some months beforehand.

Saturday, 25 September dawned and we headed off early to the Thalwil Spital, for the baby to be induced, whilst we knew our families back home were sitting down to a Grand Final football game between Carlton and Hawthorn. Both of us were totally unprepared by any birth classes. The local classes were all in German and mine only stretched to theological discourse. Merridie preferred to read a few books. But nothing in print can prepare one for what birth entails. After eight long hours of painful labour, the Swiss doctor's broken English in the labour room did not smooth the path. He kept shouting at Merridie, 'Pull! Pull!' I looked at him, confused, and said, 'Don't you mean push?' to which he would wave his hand dismissively and say, '*Jawohl*. . . push!' What seemed like a further eternity passed. Suddenly, the baby appeared, blue and bloody. I admit now I got the biggest shock of my life. It was a 4.6 kg girl. I know my first words were, 'What's this, Doctor?' The doctor mumbled something about everyone making mistakes. I named her Claire. Merridie was overcome with surprise, especially holding a red-haired daughter some thirteen years after she had lost her vibrant red-haired mother to cancer. I remember driving back to the Seminary later and finding myself stunned and speechless when it came to describing what we'd been through. I am still reminded of my reaction that night by numerous friends with long memories who now live all around the world.

Though born in Switzerland, our daughter Claire attracted no rights to citizenship, unlike a child born in Australia. We were amused to discover the extraordinary lengths to which one must go to be entitled to such civil rights. A continuous residency, not just in the country but in the one canton, for some ten years was required. Then the cultural tests were applied. Some were sensible, such as fluency in the language and a working knowledge of the history and social customs. Others were extreme. These demanded a familiarity with the local dialect and included a visit to one's home to inspect it for cleanliness and 'Swissness'. In addition, friends and acquaintances needed to attest to one's cultural assimilation.

Later, as a mayor in St Kilda who inducted many migrants into Australian citizenship, I was to muse on the striking difference between Swiss practice and the multiculturalism we embrace in Australia. We require nothing in terms of proficiency in the English language, let alone anything as intrusive as home cleanliness or as quixotic as competence in that nasal branch of English known as the Aussie dialect.

These experiences of being an outsider, essentially tolerated but never made welcome in the Swiss culture, were formative for later work and understanding. Unless you have experienced the equivocating, suspicious attitude of authorities toward you, it is hard to imagine the sense of anxiety and fear of rejection with which so many migrants constantly live. Begrudging, conditional acceptance is unsatisfying and makes one feel second-class.

Life in a Swiss seminary

—

Equally important in shaping our cultural perspectives was the exposure to fellow students. We had come from a Baptist background that seemed to name the obvious sins as drinking, gambling and sexual immorality. We grew up believing that, if one was personally converted, then intuitively one would act justly.

I remember being shocked at university to discover that Christians could be just as oppressive as atheists, communists, humanists or anyone else. My assumption that a Christian faith automatically guaranteed a disposition towards justice and compassion was shaken. To be confronted at university with inescapable facts that the murderous racism of apartheid in South Africa had been devised by Christians, bolstered with theological explanations and maintained by a parliamentary regime made up of professing believers, was shattering. How could this be if they were true followers of Jesus of Nazareth?

The orthodox categories of what behaviour defined a Christian and what did not continued to be challenged at the seminary in Rueschlikon. To our amazement, we found that the Italian Baptist students all voted communist in Italian elections. In their opinion, only the communists had the discipline to clean up the political corruption collusively maintained by the major party (the Christian Democrats) and the Mafia. Similarly, many East European pastors were very loyal to the communist party—more out of fear, but some genuinely believed in a system which had been all they had known. Some Scandinavian Baptists, to our way of thinking, had positively bohemian moral views when it came to sex and censorship. British Baptists loved their Queen and their sherry. We Australian Baptists loved and saluted the Crown, but the sherry was seen by most as a secret pleasure in our antipodean, Baptist, teetotalling world.

This vigorously pressed the question of faith and culture, belief and behaviour. Was there any given correspondence between them? Were the norms of Christian practice to conveniently conform to the quirks of local custom? This has become a perennial search, well brought out in our quest for Christian authenticity back in St Kilda. Facing these issues whilst in our training years was extremely valuable.

Studying the Bible in its original languages, Hebrew and

Greek, was a scholarly cross-cultural discipline. But studying it with seminarians from other continents and cultures marvellously enlarged the horizon. Whatever the ancient biblical writers intended, we discovered that every culture makes its own interpretation. The Italian students were always attuned to the revolutionary nuances and preferred a Jesus in Che Guevara garb. A Balinese student opened up the New Testament textual possibilities of the 'rocks crying out' which resonated with an animistic world back in Bali. The Africans never failed to observe the unmistakable struggle against imperialism in Jesus, a Jew, being executed by imperial Rome. One professor, Dr Thorwald Lorenzen, whose lectures in systematic theology I found especially insightful, became a close friend and mentor. It was his subjects on human rights and ethics in particular that focussed my interest in the direction of a politico/theological critique. He was to supervise the treatise I completed in my final year.

Living in Central Europe we discovered that we became patriotic to the point of foolishness. I kept reminding our European colleagues that we were the only country in the world that occupied a whole continent to ourselves. I reminded the Swiss that we had more snow in Australia than in all of Switzerland, but had to fudge when they enquired how come I could not ski.

The acme for our gushing nationalism was Australia's victory in the America's Cup. In ecstatic, vicarious joy, I raced around the college grounds and put Aussie flags in the hands of all the garden gnomes and statues. I placed a huge painted sign on the student noticeboard proclaiming 'Australia Rules: OK!'

I was terribly deflated when a sleepy Texan, watching this burst of patriotism with cynical detachment, asked what the hell I was doing. I explained that a historic victory over the money and might of that sailing Goliath, America, had been won by a little battler down under. He sarcastically drawled, 'Well, y'all get tired of anything after 135 years!'

It was always deflating to realise that Australia was an insignificant power player. Precisely because we did not threaten anyone, an Australian often ended up as president of the student body. Most Europeans had little comprehension of Australia other than a gaping, empty space filled with kangaroos and cuddly koalas. One Nigerian student called Johnston became a special friend and, as we were leaving for home after having spent much time telling him about Australia, he said to us, 'Drive home carefully.'

Some of the European students were certainly wary of each other and everyone was wary of the Americans. Their naive blundering emanated from an assumption that we all felt unfeigned, spontaneous gratitude for their nation's momentous contribution to global freedom and truth. The diet of US civil religion that they imbibed with their mother's milk had taught them to believe that America had a God-given messianic destiny to save the world from communism. The problem was that they were fanatically intent on saving us whether we wanted to be saved or not. The American students soon discovered that even their allies could be as cold as the freezing Cold War reality.

For some of the American professors, particularly the visiting ones, this was even harder. They were not used to the European/Australian way of teachers being adjudged by the content of their courses and not merely by their seniority or number of degrees. A few who taught us unpleasantly faced their nemesis under the glaring and ruthless scrutiny of some very intelligent students.

There was a nuclear despair that infected our peers. We met many young couples who had chosen not to have children because they believed a nuclear war was probable. They lived with the conviction that the theatre for this conflagration was Europe—namely, their backyard. It was the Germans who expressed their boiling anger and helplessness the most. This was understandable when one realised that the West Germans had most of NATO's nuclear warheads on their soil without any control over the trigger. That prerogative belonged to NATO and particularly the Americans, whose missiles pointed menacingly at Moscow and East Germany. Mirroring them were the Warsaw Pact weapons, many deployed on East German soil and most locked onto West German targets. The control of these death weapons was wrested out of East German hands and entrusted to Moscow. A divided Germany provided the bull's-eye in the target for Europe's geo-political brinkmanship and battle of nerves.

The romantic, distant continent of Australia seemed a world away from this surreal madness. Our image was of hazy summer days where Aussies would still be rolling on the suntan oil and saluting each other with 'No worries, mate' as clouds of nuclear fallout billowed across Europe.

In that angry climate, we studied with some urgency the need to find a reconciling ethic. A compelling edge to our academic pursuits was the expression of a multicultural community. Could we live in harmony as a signpost to the polarised Cold War blocs? Could our unity in Christ transcend political and cultural differences? The descent into cultural stereotyping was often unexpectedly rapid. Just below the surface still simmered the hostilities of our parents' generation, who fought a bloody world war and constructed caricatures of their opponents known as *fiend bilde* (enemy pictures).

We painfully discovered that building trust and community in an international community—even one sharing a common faith—is no simple task. Stripped of the cultural cues you rely on at home, misunderstandings arise effortlessly. It is amazing how such fundamental dimensions as humour can contribute to community building or to its destruction. Regrettably, there is no such thing as a cross-cultural joke. Well-intentioned attempts at humour usually end up being totally miscontrued by someone.

Language is mystifying. We sang 'Waltzing Matilda' one night as an Aussie contribution to a social night, only to have a puzzled Hungarian student say the expression 'when my billy boils' embarrassed him because in his language a billy is a chamber pot.

As the part-time English teachers, we constantly had to stifle laughter. I asked the class to put the word 'adult' in a sentence and an East German student proudly asked to read his sentence, as he had used it in the plural. He read out: 'My daughter goes to evening classes for adultery.' I suggested that we don't need classes for that in the West.

Our regular escape from the pressures of study was our English-speaking church in Lucerne. We made some good, non-theological friends there. I was inducted as the pastor, a part-time position, in July 1981. The forty-minute drive from Zurich that we took each week was one of the highlights of our time there. If only all trips to church were just as scenic, then church growth and renewal would be a sure thing.

Our church secretary was an American who had worked for years as an attendant in Disneyland. He had settled in, Switzerland because it was the only country in the world that was like a permanent Disneyland: no crime and beautifully clean. He wore a Mickey Mouse watch and had a Mickey Mouse telephone. Unfortunately, he also professed a Mickey Mouse faith. He would passionately pray for the Reagan government that represented Christ in the world and was faithfully fighting the Devil, namely the Soviets.

I guess all this was a bit much for me, particularly when it was less than a year after a Baptist leader, President Jimmy Carter, whom I deeply admired, had been electorally humiliated at the hands of this new 'Christ figure', President Reagan, whom I deeply distrusted. Politics, gospel and pastoral care for those whose worldview disturbed me were intertwined in this, my first pastoral ministry. They are the same tensions which continue to intrigue me even now in a totally different context.

It is to this church experience of pastoral care of a motley bunch of South Africans, Kiwis, Brits, Yankees and most other English-*sprechende* peoples that I owe some of my formative insights. They argued, laughed and lunched every Sunday after the worship service at Die Drei Könige hotel; they were thrown together from a host of denominations and united in the company of Christ. Against the beautiful and imposing giant of Mount Pilatus, which tradition taught was the suicide place of Pontius Pilate who condemned Christ, we found comfort and security. Our daughter Claire was dedicated in a memorable service there and my sermonic yodelling was graciously accepted by a patient congregation as ministry.

Part of our hearts stayed in the Lucerne Christian Fellowship. How could I ever forget the morning after a service when our Disneyland church secretary asked if anyone would like to feed the remaining communion bread to the ducks in Lake Lucerne? You can imagine how the Catholics in our congregation reacted.

In that church was Beat, the first schizophrenic person I had to try to understand and pastorally support. I found him scary and unpredictable. The time he was hospitalised, I visited the forbidding eighteenth-century institution and shrank back in fear at the dishevelled wild inmates who looked feral and murderous. It was the first psychiatric hospital I had ever entered and I was so uncomfortable that I stayed there barely any time. Little was I to know that psychotic people were to become a major responsibility in my future ministry, and a future friendship circle.

Beat invited Merridie and me to lunch one Sunday. He had no idea of cleanliness or cooking. Thinking back now to the way we looked into his gangrenously dirty coffee cups, I realise how we were both being prepared for what St Kilda would hold. We've seen a few cups since then that looked much worse.

Life and faith in communist Eastern Europe
⤚

Every summer we made a trip into Eastern Europe, then still solidly communist and atheist by creed. We discovered communities united by fear of ideological and totalitarian governments. Though we travelled and preached in the churches of many different socialist countries, it was the Romanians who claimed a special affection in our hearts. We would pack our cases with Bibles and biblical commentaries, as they were starved of resources for their burgeoning churches.

The border crossings were always a nightmare as we sweated on the inspection that would reveal a load of contraband, subversive literature. Our ploy was always the same. An Australian passport was such a novelty that they were easily distracted and easily suborned when we produced toy kangaroos and presented them as gifts. Watching their delight and madness in hopping like a kangaroo convinced us that the communist system was not impregnable.

Our first trip in, though, was not quite as smooth. At that time Merridie was three months into her first pregnancy, so we decided to book a sleeper for her whilst I 'toughed out' the night sitting up. We spent a magical day walking around Budapest, a truly beautiful city, before we boarded the train headed for Bucharest. In the wee small hours after crossing the border, Merridie's sleeper was invaded by two huge Romanian guards, one a woman, whose bulk filled the little cabin. Whilst not understanding any of the interchange, it was obvious to Merridie that the two Hungarian women in the two other bunks were being given a very hard time. The animosity between the two nationalities was clearly apparent.

They then turned their attention to Merridie and all she understood was 'passport', which she duly found and presented. The guards were none too impressed that in their hands they held my passport, which Merridie had mistakenly grabbed before I left her there. They insisted on a baggage search and again distrust showed in their faces, as Merridie's bags held numerous cartons of Kent cigarettes which our friends had pleaded with us to bring, for they formed the most useful means of exchange in Romania. She tried to explain she had a *Mann* on the train who smoked a lot, and so, in a flimsy body-clinging nightie, with two huge guards brandishing rifles behind her, she had to walk the length of the train looking for me, opening every compartment door, to the chagrin of sleeping occupants. I had wisely gone right to the far end, had a whole compartment to myself and was soundly asleep when a shaking and shaken Merridie opened the door and fell on me. We got out of that one and my case with all the books wasn't even checked. Merridie, however, resolutely refrained from accompanying me on the two further trips that I took there.

The Romanians had a romantic charm and Latin chaos that overflowed into their worship. Services would last two hours and, besides the angelic music, the most breathtaking feat was watching young children sit demurely and perfectly still throughout the whole period. I never did work out how they taught such obedience and I have failed to replicate that discipline in my own kids. It must be cultural. If one did not preach for at least one hour in Romania, it was not a real sermon. Men sat on one side and women, who were allowed to publicly pray but not to preach, sat on the other. Merridie was discreetly asked to take her earrings out, as only the loose women wore those.

We were never permitted to stay in private homes, as that robbed the government of valuable hard-currency tourist expenditure. Because the system was utterly corrupt we travelled the country using bulk packets of Kent cigarettes as currency. Though all medical treatment was theoretically free, the reality was you needed to bribe a doctor to get attention. The black market mysteriously dictated Kent cigarettes as the currency, and they were a gift we dispensed to our many friends with medical conditions to give them some hope. The irony of importing cancer sticks to get medical treatment never troubled Romanians. There were numerous families we visited who had enormous health problems and for us a few packets of Kents seemed such a paltry response, but the look on their faces made it feel we had delivered a miracle cure.

The hospitality of Romanians was fantastic, but agonising. Repeatedly, our hosts prepared huge meals, only to sit back and watch us eat because there was not enough food to feed everyone. This always posed the most acute of dilemmas, as not to eat and insist that those with greater need should share the food only offended their hospitality. We often felt heartbroken seeing so many children with black, rotten teeth due to a lack of milk.

Fear of the Securitate was palpable. Their presence was ubiquitous in every sector of Romanian life and easily identified, as they so often wore a uniform of shiny suit and regulation sunglasses. Preaching had to be strictly non-political. Yet, despite the monstrosities of communist leader Ceaucescu's modernisation, the spirit of the Romanians we met remained undaunted.

The courage of so many groups, including the churches, to provide an alternative to the State's propaganda was inspiring. We observed first-hand the highly political nature of proclaiming that Jesus is Lord and so, by implication, the first secretary of the communist party is not. The cost of this confession was not unlike that facing the first believers in imperial Rome, when they refused to greet others with the salute that Caesar is Lord.

Rapid growth of the churches provoked close scrutiny and suspicion from the government. International links which Christian relationships bring were always regarded as potentially subversive. The remarkable growth of the free churches in places like Romania and Russia was due to the prominence of preaching. It provided a legitimate platform for an alternative vision to the stale, repressive State message of magnificent socialist advances. In these states, the Orthodox Church had virtually abandoned preaching, and its worship was a liturgy magnificent in mystery but marginalised in articulating an ethic of resistance. Of course, any group that grew rapidly was keenly watched by the Department of Cults. It was a potential political rival to the party and harassment and persecution were as routine in church experience as the sacrament.

Perhaps our most poignant experiences were the three times we drove into East Germany to visit and stayed with two families there. My rudimentary German and their attempts at English made it a learning experience in more ways than one.

We were moved by the awful choices young people had to make in their teenage years in East Germany. It was a Lutheran country, the birthplace and loyal territory of Martin Luther himself. The communists were not at all against cashing in on the Protestant pilgrims like us who visited Wittenberg, despite their ideological contempt for this class enemy of the peasants who had advocated their bloody suppression in the revolt in 1534 CE. The communists produced a magnificent party for Luther's 450th birthday that rolled in the hard currency.

Ever since Luther's reformation, over eighty per cent of Germans in East Germany had taken a Lutheran confirmation service at fourteen. The socialist State had determined that they needed to neutralise this superstition and so devised a parallel socialist confirmation service. Preparation for an oath of atheism and allegiance to the socialist State was undertaken at school under the supervision of teachers.

Annette was the daughter of a Baptist pastor who was one of our East German friends. We had met her father when he came to a one-month theological program one summer at our seminary. He had pleaded with us to visit them and to bring some hope and encouragement to the young in his church. Annette was academically brilliant and had long cherished a desire to become a medical doctor. But she was confronted with a cruel choice that was to test her faith. If a student refused to take the socialist and atheist oath, then they could effectively forget entrance into any prestigious university faculty. In the church, many Christian parents believed that this oath was only a form of words and one could rationalise that the secret belief within the heart was true faith. Others, like

Annette, believed that this constituted the core of credible faith. If it never cost, then it never really counted.

In our trips over three successive summers we watched her anguish, her personal courage and her freedom as she refused to participate. Annette was blocked from medicine despite her excellent grades and has pursued her faith in training to be a deaconess. She is now involved in ministry to many in need and is married with two children.

We will never forget the parting we had with that family, all weeping as we bade farewell before crossing through the Wall. To them, it was the Wall symbolising their entrappedness. They spoke to us of *Mauer-krankheit* (Wallsickness). Little did any of us dream that within six years the Wall would come tumbling down and they would all be able to travel to oft-dreamed-of places in Western Europe.

The beginning of the end

⟶

All too soon, the three-and-a-half years of theological study finished. I completed a Bachelor of Divinity and was graduating at the end of April 1984. Merridie completed two years' worth and planned to finish her studies later in Melbourne.

We had explored options of going into the inner city of Melbourne to begin simultaneously a law practice and a church ministry. Our superintendent of the Baptist denomination in Melbourne could not see any spot for us. In a throwaway line he said, 'Of course there is always St Kilda, but you would not want to go there.' That was intriguing and provocative. Anything that bad had to be worth a try. He dissuaded us with reminders that the denomination thought it such a struggling church that it should be closed and its property assets realised to assist more productive and growing churches.

We thanked him for his assistance and began some correspondence with a church that had fifteen to twenty attendees. Our contemporaries at Rueschlikon were receiving their calls from churches in their home countries. Often they came as a professional dossier detailing the church goals, local history, manse proportions and salary terms and conditions.

Ours came in a letter from St Kilda Baptist Church on a half-sheet of paper consisting of little more than a sentence which said they wanted us to consider coming to pastor the church. There was no manse; all they could offer was a flat and enough to pay us for one day a week.

I remember showing our scrappy letter of call to colleagues at the seminary and watching the amazement on their faces as they commented on how differently Australian churches do it. But it sparked something within us. From our superb outlook across to the Swiss Alps, we wrote back and said, 'Yes, we're interested. We'll be home in July to talk it over in more detail.'

Leaving Rueschlikon was not easy. Merridie and I were both exhausted after a frantic last semester in which I completed a thesis—'The Politics of Jesus: An Analysis of the Writings of John H. Yoder'. I also crammed for a two-hour oral examination in which I knew I would be asked to translate unsighted passages of Hebrew and Greek and then to recall information from tomes of systematic theology and Church history. On top of that, we were enduring constant broken nights typical of life with a lively eighteen-month-old. Merridie was also three months into her second pregnancy.

The long winter of 1983–84 had confirmed to us we were ready to return home and to leave the pressure of study to our more academic friends who had dug in for a PhD, with a future in theological teaching in their sights. Nevertheless, it was hard to leave some good friends behind, knowing full well we were headed half a world away. I had thought I would go back into working in law as I still did not conceive of myself as ready to ascend to that priestly caste that ordination conferred. St Kilda, though, remained a distant and somewhat attractive possibility for the fleshing out of some of the longings for an alternative style of ministry that continued to ferment within us. We actually had no specific place to call home. At that point, and from that distance, Australia seemed enough.

My parents flew over for my graduation and joined us for the next few months on our last lap of travelling. We flew to Israel on 25 April and had ten wonderful days in that history-steeped country. It made a lot of biblical stories come alive. For one raised on the Bible, it had the feeling of going home. Places like Bethlehem and Bethany seemed as familiar to us from tea-table talk and bedtime stories as the streets of Black-burn. Perhaps most surprising to us was how Australian the Sea of Galilee seemed. It is now surrounded by eucalyptus trees donated by Australia after Israeli nationhood in 1949 and to all intents and purposes could be a lake out the back of Bourke. It's only coming across ancient towns such as Tiberias that spoils the illusion that Jesus grew up with swooping magpies and the scent of ghost gums.

After that sojourn, Mum and Merridie stayed with friends in Switzerland whilst I took Dad into Romania for my last visit. It was again a moving encounter with their religious zeal and uncertain political contingencies. Dad found himself preaching at all hours of the day, for our friends wanted to get the most out of all visitors. It was a tearful goodbye as deep down we knew it might be a lifetime before we met again.

One of my friends was a pastor in volatile Sibiu, where so

many Germans had found themselves trapped on the wrong side of Churchill's aptly named iron curtain that they had settled in and formed a *Deutsche-sprechende* church. I had preached there in German and this minister tenderly informed me that he would name his soon-to-be-born child Timothy if it was a boy, in order to remember my visits. And so he did. Such was the importance of a window into the West.

A glimpse of the American soul

~

We travelled homewards via the United States of America. It was my first visit to Uncle Sam. We started out in New York in the last weeks of May and picked up a hire car which took the five of us over much of the continent. It was six weeks of unrelenting heat. Never, ever, have we felt so thankful for air-conditioning in a car. I also saw quite clearly why Americans have shopping malls everywhere. They help you forget about life outside.

We enjoyed the hospitality of a number of welcoming people who shared their intimate hopes for their nation, although the practice of extending hospitality via a Diner's Card rather than in private homes struck us as a novel but less intimate approach.

One experience brought us face to face with the common American overuse of superlatives. I had been invited to briefly address an evening congregation of seven hundred or so in Texas. I had only met the senior pastor for five minutes before the service. Merridie, my parents and lively Claire were well ensconced in the congregation. The senior pastor got up and introduced me as 'the best student who has ever graduated from Rueschlikon and the finest preacher in Australia'.

Merridie and my parents burst into spontaneous laughter, only to discover they were alone in the joke. We quickly learnt not to take their hyperbole too literally.

Perhaps the most moving moment for me was sitting one evening in Martin Luther King's church in downtown Atlanta listening to Daddy King preach and later meeting Coretta and Martin Jnr. Many of the people we met were Baptists who had generously supported the seminary in Switzerland. It made us appreciative of the international fraternity to which some seventy-five million people belong.

A chance to recognise this body of Baptists came in an unusual way a few years later. I was doing a legal defence to fix a determinate sentence for a Yugoslavian double-murderer who had been sentenced for 'the term of his natural life'. He had committed the sickening crime of axing to death his de facto and her daughter, but had become a believer and was baptised as a Baptist whilst in prison. He was applying for a fixed sentence and got fourteen years rather than life. The Supreme Court judge in summing up the case made some reference to his concern that this man had joined a little-known sect—the Baptists.

I could not resist begging his indulgence and then going on to explain that actually the Yugoslavian Baptist Church was part of the Baptist Union of Victoria, that it was a constituent member of the Australian Baptist Union that belongs to the Baptist World Alliance, of which there are around seventy-five million members, making it one of the largest Protestant churches in the world. Some of its better known members, I went on to say, were ex-President Jimmy Carter, Martin Luther King and Jesse Jackson. The judge graciously excused himself and concluded in a somewhat less strident tone that obviously it was only a little-known sect to him.

In our American journeyings, we came to understand the reservoir of civic pride that commonly expressed itself in religious aspirations. A religious idiom claimed public discourse from presidents and politicians to leaders in business, art and entertainment. They felt comfortable in appealing to traditions laid out in the first sermons of their pilgrim fathers. The notion of America as a light in a dark place and a city set on a hill has continued to inspire patriotism and loyalty since the day this sermon was first preached by the pilgrim father, the Reverend John Winthrop. This dream is still appealed to and gives a cause and energy to American national pride.

Of course, this was unfamiliar to our Aussie ears. At home, a prime minister speaking publicly about private faith was unimaginable. It would be an electoral liability because people would assume that he or she was a religious fanatic. As we later witnessed, the overflow of private faith and civic religion into global politics did become dangerous and fanatical when President Bush spoke in holy-war language of praying for a military victory in a Christian versus Muslim conflict as he announced the Gulf War campaign.

On 7 July 1984 we arrived back in Melbourne. The grey, overcast day did nothing to dampen our spirits. It was good to be back. Our families were at the airport and Claire's first words were to Merridie's brother Harley, "Ow ya doin', 'Arley?' with a distinct American drawl she had picked up. We felt disorientated and somewhat homeless, but it didn't seem to matter. We knew the future would unfold in its own good time.

three

Finding a place to call home

In mid-July 1984 we set foot in St Kilda. It was a Sunday, so we pulled up outside the Baptist chapel in a bleak street surrounded by warehouses and heard beer-bottle glass crunching under the car's front tyres. Sitting out on the curb at the front of The Queens Arms Hotel diagonally opposite the church was a drunk feverishly clutching a bottle in a paper bag. It was a miserably cold day and the street was a mess of broken-up pavement and scattering papers from the local factories. A strangled melaleuca tree was the only green vegetation bravely resisting the asphalt bedding.

Inside the church was an equally uninspiring picture. A small congregation of twenty mainly elderly people were gathered on hard wooden pews designed to mortify the flesh, and symmetrically scattered as distant from each other as the pew placement would allow. Church appeared to be a private event to endure in isolation rather than in communal closeness.

It was the cold that hit us first. Although it had been much colder in Switzerland, everything was centrally heated and gloves and coats were never far away. Not so in Melbourne, where the absence of snow deluded us into thinking it was never really cold, but where winter's cold winds would regularly cut us up. The church was without any adequate heating and the bare floorboards were riddled with holes. Unholy draughts of cold air blasted throughout the building, challenging concentration and perseverance in worship.

The preacher was Dr Peter Broughton, an interim minister who had come for three months and stayed for three years. He did not live in the area, but faithfully turned up to preach on Sundays. It had been this style of ministry that had kept the doors open for many years. In fact, he had encouraged the church to undertake a faith venture and to buy the block of flats right next door. Three banks had laughed at the prospect, but eventually they did it with gifts from within the Baptist Union and the proceeds from the old church manse that had been sold when the church secretary had a fit of depression about its upkeep back in the early 1970s.

The church congregation had not known a full-time minister for over twenty years and had relied upon student and interim ministers to survive. In the process it had become wary and untrusting of so many novel ideas that enthusiastically flowed from student pastors. It had soon twigged that theological students had no real intention of hanging around and seeing these ideas through. They were just practising before seeking a secure stipend and 'real church'.

The first morning we visited, Dr Broughton preached a magnificent sermon of hope from the prophet Isaiah. He struck a chord with us by quoting, 'Remember not the former things. Behold, I am doing something new.' We certainly hoped that these words would become prophetic in our experience. They ignited a confirmation of the call we were feeling. We sensed him handing on the baton, even though we had not formally accepted.

A few conversations later with the congregation assured us that they would not resist experimental forms of ministry and that they would embrace change with our ministry. We then agreed to accept the call of the church. I needed to do three days a week as a lawyer in the firm I had worked with in suburban Box Hill before we left for overseas in order to supplement what the church could afford to pay me. So from the very outset I had the perception that my approach to ministry was as a worker-priest.

Moving in
—

Probably the hardest bit of reality hit us when we were shown through the flat next to the church that was to be our accommodation. Tenants had just recently left and every room had walls caked with thick nicotine residue. In fact everything, including the light shades, looked a deep yellow, but was found to be white once scrubbed. The bathroom sinks were irremediably stained and there were no floor coverings. Merridie's nesting instincts, with our second child's birth just some six weeks away, went into a spin. We drove back the fifteen kilometres to my parents' home and hardly spoke to each other. We discovered quickly that a small inner-city church has little able-bodied 'man'-power. Everything was left to a few women, and a job like renovating a flat was extremely taxing both physically and financially.

But somehow over the next several weeks, we were helped in doing a clean-up job and a friend and I enjoyed assaulting the nicotine with fresh paint. New carpets went down and, with a bit of work in the bathroom, it was pretty liveable by the time we moved in after Elliot's arrival.

Unlike his sister's, Elliot's birth went smoothly and it was a joy to welcome another large and healthy child. He arrived in the world beaming and we have often commented since on him being the 'child of our depression'. Over the next few months, in the midst of some bleak patches for us both whilst we struggled to cope with change, grieved the loss of our moorings and faced the fears of failure, Elliot ministered sheer well-being.

My first Bible study at the church, the first Wednesday evening after we moved into the flat, almost finished me off. I had picked up the Bible text they were studying that week and studiously prepared a message that drew on my Hebrew and the subtle nuances from a scholarly reading of the commentaries. I was keen to impress and carefully laid out the exegetical meaning, demonstrating how a classical education overseas was able to marshall the latest scholarship to enrich our learning. I paused and opened all this up for discussion.

There followed an awkward silence. Finally, one of the five elderly members turned to me and said, 'Well, don't expect me to contribute. I left my hearing aid at home and have not heard a thing you said.' That prompted the next to say, 'I've brought the wrong pair of glasses and haven't even found where it is in the Bible yet.' Quickly the next woman said that she and Ces were out very late last night and were too tired to follow all this. I walked back to our flat deflated that this was the pinnacle of four years of disciplined study. Rueschlikon hadn't prepared me for this.

Even in my first weeks of preaching, I felt like my words were falling to the ground like overripe tomatoes. I had developed a style suited to preaching in chapel services for a theological seminary, but the content and approach left a look of death in the eyes I faced. My sister Janet, who came to our church to support us, told me I sounded like a cross between an English toff and a German theologian and I needed to get back to a bit of reality.

So I consciously tried to drop the articulated accent or 'toffiness' I had mastered for teaching English in Europe. It had been essential because my Australian nasal drawl could not be understood in middle-Europe. On top of that, I under-took a re-Aussification of my nuances and a deconstruction of my heady theological framework. It seemed to work. Within a few months, there were even smiles of response and laughter at the lighter touches I interweaved. I could tell that for the most part the crew were pretty much with me.

St Kilda: a tale of two cities

Here we were supplanted in a part of Melbourne that was as foreign to us as all of Europe had been four years previously. Its street language was more impenetrable than high German and its subcultures centred on esoteric value codes with their own music, dress sense and hang-outs. So the need for orien-tation was real.

We began to see that St Kilda had many different faces, but two stood out. The first was the opulence, wealth and prestige of some of the lifestyles that have regarded, still do regard, St Kilda as home. This was epitomised in the mansions on St Kilda Hill. The second was the poverty, social isolation and meagreness of the forgotten people—the many gutsy bat-tlers who also have lived and continue to live there. They lived in the valley. Rich and poor lived side by side without the presence of a middle class made of families. The growing economic and social gap in the nation between rich and poor was anticipated in St Kilda. It was a glimpse of the future divide in the country.

As the official St Kilda historian A. Longmire has said, the homes on St Kilda Hill were first built at the height of a frenzied, no-holds-barred building boom during the 'marvellous Melbourne' outpouring of wealth. The city of St Kilda offered some of the most magnificent homes in Melbourne. Mansions like Oberwyl in Burnett Street boasted thirty-six rooms, a ballroom, a parapet roof, ornate Victorian decoration, and secret chambers and solid wooden shutters to provide protection against bushrangers. The council building was a breathtaking boom-style palace designed by William Pitt and built just before the 1890s depression hit. Whilst it is one of the most eyecatching pieces of town-hall architecture in Melbourne, the depression robbed it of an extravagant grand tower that would have capped an extraordinary building.

Mayoral functions were always grand, as befitted such an important wealthy city, and the mayoral allowance was second only to the City of Melbourne. Councillors grew accustomed to enjoying the best imported whiskies and cigars at civic functions. St Kilda Pier was the first greeting point for regal parties. Lord Hopetoun, who opened the first Australian parliament in 1901, was welcomed to the country at St Kilda Pier by the Mayor of St Kilda before travelling to Melbourne to preside over the birth of a modern nation.

The removal of threats of bushrangers in the 1880s cleared the way for the gentry to claim St Kilda as their French Riviera. Its beautiful beach was the closest to Melbourne and horse-and-carriage access ensured that it was an elite refuge. Only day-trippers could commute to St Kilda until the advent of the cable car in the early 1900s. Architect Carlo Catani remodelled the foreshore to resemble a European resort, with a split-level esplanade running along the beach and foreshore. Californian date palms along this magnificent boulevarde mixed the cultural metaphor. St Kilda was known as Toff Town. (Perhaps I was well suited here after all.)

Nineteenth-century hotels with private bathrooms, pressing rooms for lady guests, and reading and writing rooms were abundant. The George Hotel in Fitzroy Street was known as Australia's finest hotel in the nineteenth century. It had a marble entrance, banquet hall, ballroom and free garaging for the guests. High cuisine, tennis courts, croquet lawns, and billiard and smoking rooms adorned these many hotels that made St Kilda the giddy social pinnacle of Melbourne.

But it was Luna Park that forever transformed the face of St Kilda. It was the greatest amusement park in the world when it opened in 1912. Mr Moon with his rolling eyes and a toothy laugh was borrowed from Mr Moon at Coney Island, New York. Luna Park was marvellous in its scope and included the Palace of Illusions, Theatre Comique, Globe of Death, Indian Dart Gallery, River Caves, Scenic Railway (which is still operative), Palm-reading Machine, the Curious Flea Circus and the American Bowl Slide. Each year, the Luna Park Company introduced new attractions, such as the Dodgems and Big Dipper. The Luna Park slogan was 'Just for Fun'. This was the biggest thing for rocking conservative, staid Melbourne, renowned as the city of prudes.

Next door, the same company built in 1913 a theatre holding over 3000 people called the Palais de Danse, amidst churchmen and councillors raging about the temptations of the tango and the corruption of public morals. Soon theatres, music halls and entertainment centres were springing up like mushrooms throughout St Kilda. The Mayfair Theatre, Earls Court, the Victory, the Broadway, the Memorial Theatre, the St Kilda

Theatre and Palais Pictures opened to embrace the hunger for frivolity.

This displeased many of the snobbish segments of Melbourne society who believed the mass entertainment facilities to be vulgar. Disquieted, they left St Kilda for more elite and unadulterated suburbs. But they came back, as all Melburnians do, to walk into a lovely sunset, an experience offered in a jaunt out along the St Kilda Pier to Kirby's Kiosk.

The largest minority group was the Jewish community. They saw St Kilda as the most prestigious address in town and were deeply proud of their Anglo–Jewish conservatism. The Byzantine-style synagogue which opened in St Kilda in 1926 included some of Melbourne's wealthy and venerable Jewry. Australia's first Australian-born Governor General, Sir Isaac Isaacs, opposed by King George V, was one of St Kilda's proud sons and a member of the Hebrew congregation in the city. Another Hebrew synagogue St Kilda boy, Sir Zelman Cowen, would follow forty-five years later as Australian Governor General. But not all Jews were rich and some were unable to afford their seat rents by 1930. Others led secular lives and still others sought a relaxed religious emphasis. A liberal synagogue called Temple Beth Israel, the first successful liberal congregation in Australia, was established in St Kilda and brought out an American rabbi to minister to the congregation.

The first Jewish mayor anywhere in Australia was in St Kilda, establishing its acceptance of this minority that was strictly excluded from that most elite of all clubs, the Melbourne Club. It is a delight to wander down Acland Street on a Sunday morning and watch ruddy-faced East European Jews in tieless shirts buttoned right to the top furiously debating Stalin's and Krushchev's legacies, alternating between English, Yiddish and Russian. The passion is still alive.

Today, in St Kilda's most conservative Jewish quarter, huge banners hang on the main arteries announcing '*Moshiach* [Messiah] is coming. Let's be ready!' A free information telephone number invites the curious to learn how to recognise him and explains how he is on the cusp of returning. The *Lubbavitcher*, brilliantly described in Chaim Potok's books, wear their thick Russian fur hats, black robes and white leggings. Others wear their black pork-pie hats, and black suits with scruffy tassels hanging down under the jacket.

One of the women in our church was the local hairdresser and she trimmed the Jewish women's wigs to provide a natural look. Underneath the wig was the shorn hair of the married Jewish woman, which complied with the religious law's teaching of modesty and respect for one's husband. Homes are equipped with timers to switch on the lights at dark on the sabbath, and I have been requested to change a light bulb on the sabbath because respect for the sabbath's sacredness means no work must be peformed by a Jew. Modern technology has been cleverly harnessed to serve the strict religious duties without cramping lifestyles.

The second face of St Kilda was infamous for its underbelly—its sly-grog shops, illegal drugs and prostitution. Cocaine was favoured by those who could obtain it and St Kilda became the place to buy and sell it. It was used during World War I as an analgesic and became a more fashionable drug than alcohol for those who could afford it. The police reported in March 1930 that more cocaine was sold in St Kilda than anywhere else in Australia, with most of it coming from the East via Sydney. It was known as 'two-bob Joe Blow' or 'snow' and exorbitant profits were being made by its distributors. Some St Kilda pharmacies were raided and a few chemists charged. Prostitution added to St Kilda's image woes and was an evil corollary of the good times that mass entertainment afforded.

These were the more malignant examples of the other St Kilda. The benign strand was the erection of acres of new affordable housing, comprising workmen's cottages and flats that housed at first the servants of the gentry and then the workers who serviced Melbourne's nearby port and trams. These lower classes inhabited the valley and trudged up to the hill to offer their domestic skills to the lords of the manors.

A St Kilda hero

～

It was the Great Depression years that threw up St Kilda's first champion in local politics. His story has been a source of great inspiration to me and is movingly related in Longmire's third volume of St Kilda's official history. His name was Albert Jacka and he succeeded in becoming mayor in 1930 at the beginning of the Great Depression.

He had already become an Australian icon due to his war exploits. He was the first Australian to be awarded the country's highest military award for heroism, the Victoria Cross, in World War I. He saw his last four mates killed or wounded at Courtney's Post at Gallipoli on 19 May 1915, when the battalion was attacked by Turkish troops who captured some twelve metres of the Australian line. When he saw the Turks, he shot five and killed the remaining two with his bayonet. He then applied for entry to officer training and was refused at first because he lacked a university education. He persisted and was eventually admitted and topped the graduate course.

He left for France and, in the judgment of war historian C.E.W. Bean, his endeavours at Pozieres and at Bullecourt should have earned him another two Victoria Crosses rather than the Military Cross and Bar he was awarded.

Jacka was embarrassed to return home in 1918 to a hero's welcome and a convoy of eighty-five cars which placed Jacka at the head and took him to meet the Governor General. He was awarded a gold watch and $500 from the notorious businessman, John Wren. Out of largesse, which he lavished extensively around Melbourne at the time, Wren set Jacka up in an electrical business, and then Jacka entered local council as a St Kilda councillor.

In 1929 Wren withdrew his support when it was rumoured that Jacka had refused to take a course of political action that Wren wanted. Jacka commented that he preferred to be closed down than to allow Wren to think he had bought him. His firm went into liquidation just at the time he was about to become mayor. This coincided with the bitter onset of the Depression. Many returned soldiers and families were in financial strife and petitioned the council for relief. The humiliation and hunger was degrading and many pleaded with council to hold off on collecting the rates until they found employment. Others begged council to employ them so that they might feed their families and pay their rents.

Most expected governments to steer them through hard times to safety, but they were in for a shock. The economic wisdom of this pre-Keynesian era was for balanced budgets, which cruelly dictated cuts in spending and welfare. Mayor Jacka took an opposite view and, though his pecuniary circumstances forced him to move out of his own home through unemployment, he dedicated himself to fight the economic chaos for his constituents with the same valour and determination he had shown in the trenches fifteen years earlier.

He strengthened the St Kilda unemployment organisation,

funnelling council funds and using his mayoral car to collect food donated by the St Kilda stallholders and distribute it to the hungry. He convinced council to establish a boot-repairing depot based at the Town Hall. He knew from observation that the unemployed trudged many miles barefoot, or with shoes lined with cardboard, looking for work. Boots were just as necessary as food for the unemployed, who hit the wallaby track with no promise of a place to doss down.

All this was at some political risk as it was the ratepayers, not tenants or the poor, who elected councils. They steadfastly believed that council expenditure was to maintain the value of their property. In Mayor Jacka, they discovered a voice hostile to the uncaring rich and an advocate for the poor. Jacka expected governments to show the flexibility and leadership he had sought from commanding officers in the war. But to his dismay, they timidly reverted to the economic logic of increased taxes and balanced budgets, as they had done in the 1890s depression. Jacka found himself advocating the plight of tenants and putting to all local estate agents the proposal that they stay their hand for a period of one month in every case of eviction.

Of course, hardship did extend to landlords who found no rent coming in and who were dependent on that income to survive. For them, even the government's commitment to relief through welfare sustenance was viewed as a harsh imposition on taxpayers. Captain Albert Jacka died at thirty-nine years of age after a strenuous council debate on mixed bathing. His funeral cortège was one of the biggest ever seen in Melbourne, then or since, as it progressed from Melbourne Town Hall to the St Kilda cemetery. A great heart whose courage epitomised the soul of the Aussie battler was laid to rest. He is still remembered at an Australia Day service every year attended by his mayoral successors in St Kilda.

St Kilda battlers today

⟶

That face of the Aussie battler was not atypical in St Kilda. For over eighty years, St Kilda provided the cheapest flat accommodation in Melbourne. Thus, it became a magnet for the poorest and most desperate. I found myself constantly asking the question, Why is this particular person here? Most were in St Kilda for a reason. So many were refugees from mainstream Aussie existence. St Kilda was fringeland for those fleeing broken marriages, middle-class uniformity—or even the law. My legal clients seemed to include disproportionate numbers of Kiwis and Tasmanians. Jumping the Tasman or Bass Strait landed you in St Kilda. Some others were fleeing repressive regimes, particularly the Russian Jews, East Europeans and Catholic Poles. Subcultures that knew they would never be accepted in Calvinist work-ethic middle suburbia gravitated to St Kilda.

Bohemian artists, and gays unready to tell family and friends, found refuge in St Kilda's odd eccentricity. Its raffish haunts on one of Melbourne's great boulevardes, Fitzroy Street, were pure pleasure. The streets were lined with pawnshops trading cash for broken dreams, New Age bookshops, Jewish trinket stores and lots of opportunity shops. Browsing these sidewalks was a human zoo of wondrous diversity: bikini-clad girls whizzing along and terrifying pedestrians on in-line skates; punks whose purple hair and shaved forelocks raised not even an eyebrow thrashing off to their headbanging music halls of grunge and neo-gothic punk; listless druggies with dead eyes just hanging out for a fix; teenagers affixed to the serious play in the pinball parlours; and yuppies in prescription uniform of Country Road clothes, Rolex watch and BMW or Corvette.

Often they viewed each other with awe. One of Melbourne's

finest restaurants, Di Stasio, with impeccable cuisine and service, looks out onto a street where bag ladies, pimps and addicts vied for space on the footpath. Squeezing into the cracks wherever they might were street kids; homeless men with alcohol-related brain-damage, and the recently deinstitutionalised enduring the cycles of psychiatric disability.

All of these minority groups have over the years found a place of protection under St Kilda's skirts. The old lady's largesse is unfathomable. One can walk down Carlisle Street at high noon on a shopping day clothed only in a dressing gown, with hair in curlers and a cigarette hanging out of one's mouth, without a head turning. Shopkeepers know the people who genuinely need credit and give it. Others understand a psychotic episode and react maturely without hysteria. Even 'Angelo', a retarded young man who was known as a paedophile, was kept under watch by sets of stern, kindly eyes. The neighbourhood worked along informal networks that included and monitored rather than expelled.

This could never be emulated by formal social-work models that throw armies of professionals at problems, who clock off at 5.00 pm and more often than not cannot be contacted during the day because they are forever attending conferences to refine their community development skills.

St Kilda's marvellously mixed architecture has given rise to distinct settings—even ghettos. Agents will point out the differing housing markets suitable for Jews (within walking distance of a synagogue), for artists needing garrets, a block of flats for Russian *émigrés* who congregate together, enormous mansions now transmogrified into special accommodation homes for the deinstitutionalised, and small, single-fronted terraces for childless (often gay) couples.

St Kilda has its own Australian Rules football team. In a

sport-mad culture, the heart of the city resides in its sporting team. Its original playing ground was on the old bush patch where the first bushrangers regularly held up the Brighton coach and where the corroboree tree still stands. The St Kilda football team is older than the soccer teams in Italy, Germany and Argentina, and the code has been drawing some of the biggest crowds in world sport for a hundred years. Though spectacularly unsuccessful, winning only one premiership over nearly a century, St Kilda has a huge following as the social heartbeat of a flamboyant city.

The other religious centres for the poorer crowds in St Kilda are the TABs. Crowds spill out the doors and always there are those with idiosyncratic schemes for backing a sure thing—like every horse with an H as the third letter in its name. Perhaps the streaks of fatalism that infested the convicts, and the free settlers who took the gamble of leaving home and travelling 14 000 miles to the antipodes, has produced genetic traits for gambling in their descendants. Some have even contibuted to the church offering by solemnly placing their tattslotto ticket in as the plate came round.

A tale of two churches

⌁

This dualism of St Kilda's soul was manifest in her churches. In my own denomination, the first Baptist church was a magnificent large hawthorn-brick building located in a strategic place on St Kilda Hill. It was built for the opulent, who would be ministered the grace of God with the decorum appropriate to their station in life.

Australian church life had replanted the same tensions from the old country. Though they were not our religious fights and colonial life was merely inheriting the bitterness of wounds that should have healed long ago in another place, we took them up with renewed fervency.

The first Baptist church was a Particular Baptist, which meant it was strongly Calvinist in orientation. The rather noxious doctrine that defined Particular Baptists was the theory of salvation which taught that Jesus Christ only died for the Church. A shallow logic encompassed this notion: since all will not be saved, then Christ's death on Calvary is only effective for those who believe. The remainder, those outside the Church, are the objects of the wrath of God.

Gradually, being particular in theology led to being particular in practice. At first, this suited the class snobbery that was socially cohesive and instinctive to a Victorian culture on the hill. A better class of person was frequenting the chapel and socially this was not inconsistent with a particularistic theology. But society was changing and the protected environs of St Kilda Hill was being challenged by the arrival of the working classes.

The Baptist chapel warded them off with a fence around that most solemn of inner sanctuaries, the communion table. A small fence, complete with railing, communicated unmistakably that they were most particular about who might receive Christ's memorial meal. Only those whom the pastor adjudged to be in good moral standing, faith and love—that is, the elect within the elect—were granted a place at the Lord's Table. One can only surmise how much correspondence there was between such spiritual privileges and social privileges. The doctors of doctrine and moral scorekeepers were very much in control in this replication of biblical Pharisaism.

Whatever the beauty of its internal particularistic logic, this was a mean and disgraceful theology that reaped its own reward. The congregation which had had the money to erect an expensive edifice as a social statement of its power and legitimacy dwindled within forty years to a few adherents. In 1922 it closed totally and was sold, perhaps appropriately, to an equally exclusivist and particular organisation, the Masons. They continue to inhabit the building and refused me, a non-Mason, permission to enter to see the beauty of the original church. Reasons of historical sentimentality as the incumbent St Kilda Baptist minister were insufficient to warrant them revealing the exclusive and hidden mysteries of the lodge.

But down in the flood-prone valley, nestling among the workmen's cottages, was the beginning of another Baptist story. This church was despised by the Particular Baptists for its doctrinal looseness and its social laxity. On the first score, it was known as General Baptist because it had the temerity to assert that Christ died for the whole world and not just the elect, the Church. To the particular purists, this placed far too much responsibility on the free will of individuals to respond to God's grace. They much preferred a pre-cosmic election of those who were the object of God's love, as this more neatly fitted their concern to maintain God's sovereignty, even if it meant a sovereign choice of his favourites. God loving everyone and giving the life of his Son for all was cheap and plebian.

But it was to just such plebians that this valley church began to minister, contravening the principle of founding more than one Baptist church in a suburb. Its beginnings were humble. For the first thirty-five years of its life it met in halls rented from various groups, like the Australian Natives Association and the Town Hall. It eyed enviously the stature and security of the hawthorn brick on the hill. It struggled to make real the vision of a church for the ordinary, as its members had few pence for a minister's stipend and were exhausted from twelve-hour days in a six-day week of hard and unrewarding labour. Sundays were the only rest day and local parents would gladly pack the kids off and win a few precious intimate moments whilst the church ministry took Sunday school classes. Perhaps the role of sabbath school has long gone unrecognised as a striking contributor to the breeding of large families in the inner-city slums.

The big break for the church came with a new adventurous minister who in 1907, against the advice of the church leadership, went out and purchased a block of land in his own name. The risks were all his and it took another eight years before a Sunday school hall was erected on this block. It was to be the precursor to a real church when the money became available. But it never did eventuate and it was to this unrenovated Sunday school hall that we came in 1984.

However, it was not the sort of utilitarian hall that churches would normally erect for such purposes in this era. It had a magnificent stained-wood cathedral ceiling and it remains a simple sanctuary, opening one up to the wonder of the presence of God, even if an organ and stained-glass windows are missing. This little church, meeting in their Sunday school hall, was an open church in theology and practice. It became the church of tradespeople, of local children looking for something to do, and to many transients, like the sailors and soldiers during World War II who found themselves dumped at the port of Melbourne in a strange place at a strange time and who needed to hear a word of life and hope.

Perhaps the most colourful period in the church's life was under the ministry of the Reverend Duff Forbes. He was an outstanding orator whose memory for detailed biblical minutiae made him a memorable speaker and scholar. But it was to the

Jewish residents of St Kilda that he felt primarily called. He claimed to be of Jewish descent and, on the strength of that, wore a yarmulka to identify his loyalties. He committed himself to convincing any who would listen that Jesus of Nazareth was the Messiah for whom Israel was waiting.

The church became his lecture hall and drew crowds from around post-war Melbourne to hear his teaching. For many listeners the Old Testament or Hebrew scriptures came to life, and on a number of occasions he filled the huge Town Hall with crowds that included many Jews. His legacy was a mission organisation that survives today called the Jewish Evangelical Witness.

Some of the saints who were part of the story of St Kilda Baptist before our arrival were original St Kilda working people. The Bretts (father and son) had built the church. The father built the Sunday school hall in 1915 which served as the church sanctuary, whilst son Mervyn built the back hall that adjoins it some years later and which has seen many years of youth groups, play groups, and the like. Mervyn himself was a highly regarded man who led the church through many of the difficult years, putting in countless hours with groups of local young people.

Edna Brett, the daughter of Mervyn, was one of the faithful remnant keeping the doors open when we arrived. Her mother Ivy was still alive and would cheerfully shuffle in and out of the services on her walking-frame. Edna, then in her mid-sixties, loyally worked as both church secretary and treasurer. Up until just a few years before we came, she had run a youth group on Friday nights and was known to regularly vault over the horse with whoever cared to join in.

Ada Jackson was another who welcomed us warmly. She spent her whole life in St Kilda, and lived for most of her married life and widowhood in a timber house built by her grandfather in the 1860s. She spoke of sitting as a small child on the verandah, sweltering on summer evenings and watching Aboriginal campfires at what is now the council depot. Ada had been widowed after only seven years and raised her three children by taking in sewing. She was absolutely adamant that she would never leave St Kilda and her last wish came true, as she died suddenly of a heart attack at her home in 1992 at the age of eighty-two.

Another older member who made her presence felt when we arrived was Freda Ellingham. Freda was born in Inkerman Street, one of the main streets. She recalled watching the Chinese coolies driving their cattle down to St Kilda Junction. She had gone to a small private school opposite her home and worked after school in the family grocery, also in Inkerman Street. Her father was a mercenary who relished any fight, whatever the cause, wherever it was on the globe. He fought in every war from the Boer War on and was constantly away from home. Freda remembered him only vaguely. She grew up, married a fitter and turner and moved into another house in Inkerman Street. Despite the many St Kilda street names drawn from the Crimean War, such as Sebastopol, Alma and Malakof, Freda was a typical Anglo–Aussie and quite aghast and annoyed at the influx of Russian *émigrés* in her latter years. Yet the village nature of St Kilda was never more amply demonstrated than by Freda's geographic stability in living in the same street for eighty-two years.

We saw fairly early on in our ministry that Freda had her father's love of fighting. For her, it had been a lifetime of fighting with every minister's wife who had come to the church. She prided herself on this skill. For some reason, she had decided that in her eighties she was getting beyond it and that she would let Merridie become a friend. Freda eventually had to go into a nursing home when failing memory became an obvious problem and she died in 1991.

It was women such as these who had refused to listen to the prudent advice coming from the Executive Council of the Baptist Union. Discussions around the future viability of the church had gone on for some years. The old building was sitting on prime real estate. It could easily be sold off as a trendy photographer's studio, or razed and more warehouses erected in keeping with its surrounds.

But these women would hear nothing of it. This was their church. There were thousands of people living in St Kilda and they reckoned that, though it was barren soil, why should this thwart the Almighty? The fact that up to that point in time the clear sociological trend had been for the young of the church to marry and settle on quarter-acre blocks in the outer suburbs hurt, but did not deter them. They knew the needs were pressing, that other young people were moving into the inner-city, and that they had to be prepared to hand over the reins so that the church could again attract those who were genuinely seeking faith and community. So they welcomed us and a strong bond was quickly formed.

four

The church in the valley

Our ministerial stipend in 1984 for a family of four was $80 per week. There wasn't the expectation that we could save on the food bill by miraculously multiplying loaves and fishes—this was simply the outer limit of the congregation's tithing power. Unlike some other denominations that have a centralised topping-up fund, ours was the ultimate level playing field. If you could not help the church grow, then do not expect to eat. This provided gut-level incentive.

But we felt quite at peace with this prospect. We had been fully sentient, clothed and in our right minds when we accepted this call. Yes, there had been a few other calls that we had received from suburban churches with large congregations, large budgets and lovely manses, but they came unaccompanied by a still, small voice: 'This is the way, walk ye in it.' Even wise and prudent advice from our families failed to tilt the scales.

Reflecting on this faith step we took, I still wonder at the greed of some of the people on executive salaries I continually meet. So many managers are unable to measure their worth in any other terms but humungous monetary packages. Such salaries mock reason and are nonsensical, particularly when they bear such little relationship to real worth or vocation.

I ponder how much food one needs to be satisfied and healthy, how many roofs it takes to keep the rain out and provide family security. Yet houses, cars and holidays are feverishly piled up to bolster one's personal security. Commodification of personal worth has corroded the soul and debased the personally enriching notion of work as vocation. The Latin root of the word 'vocation' means *to be called*. Work, wherever possible, should embody a sense of call, as heart and body are united in contributing to society whatever the monetary reward.

To keep the wolves from the door I went back to a few days' work a week in the law. At first I would travel the twelve or so kilometres out to Box Hill to my old firm, and then later they agreed to open a branch office operating from the front rooms of the church.

So for the first six months Merridie was left in St Kilda with two young children and no familiar supports. Isolation and unfamiliarity with the networks meant both of us experienced a sense of depression. We began to discover the perimeters of the city on our doorstep. Merridie did it by walking the pram and finding the infant health centre and a few playgroups. I set out on walks or runs after work hours. As middle-class people who valued a wide range of friends and pursuits, life felt very constricted. Part of that probably had something to do with having two children demanding our attention. Merridie also often felt the lack of trees. With the memory of her childhood home of four acres in Mitcham she struggled with the vistas of rusty tin roofs and the odd strangulated tea-tree.

Doubts as to the wisdom of this call surfaced as we discovered that our lives frequently transmuted into being a door porter, responding to a never-ending series of knocks on our flat door by characters with the most unlikely stories. At any hour of the day or night, all types—from shuffling, stuttering, whisky-besotted men to flashy spivs in Al Capone cravats and lots of fast talk—would beat a path to our door. This was to prove a fast and at times bitter learning curve. Most of the stories fell into the 'new job' genre: 'I've been unemployed and just need money for a train ticket to start a new job tomorrow.' We soon learnt that the offer of a train ticket and not cash was a sure recipe for a muffled curse and hasty retreat, or a prolonged, practised response as to why cash would be more beneficial. But some of the stories broke new ground in creativity and drew my respect and admiration. They were no more honest than the 'new job' genre, but deserved a payout for sheer originality and effort.

I well remember one man who rang me from a telephone box around the corner at the St Kilda post office. He was suicidal and in tears, having arrived in St Kilda from Queensland to discover that his last family member had recently moved from the area. His story tumbled out with immense pathos and conviction. His wife and daughter had been killed when the boat they were towing had jackknifed in a tropical thunderstorm in Queensland. Guilt had engulfed him, as he had sent them off to pick up the boat knowing that his wife had qualified for a licence less than six weeks earlier. After the funeral he had entered his lounge room, seen the photos of his loved ones and hit the road to run from his guilt and grief. I was his last attempt to stare down his destructive pain, otherwise he would end it all.

I invited him around to our place, and when he saw Claire sitting at the tea table he spontaneously burst into tears. When in control of himself, he told me she reminded him of his own deceased child. He explained with enormous dignity that he knew he must turn his face homewards and go and confront his demons. No, he said, he wouldn't take any money because the last thing he had left was his pride. His story was so powerful and direct that, as I bought him a Queensland train ticket, I found myself pushing money onto him with tears streaming down my face.

That Sunday evening I related his story to a breathless congregation and we thanked God for his courage to go home and prayed for him. The next day, when I drew a total blank trying to ring the work contacts he had left with me, I felt the emptiness of realising I was a sucker. How wet behind the ears could I be? His story had been a complete charade.

Months later, I related this experience to a group of ministers meeting together in a nearby suburb. I was talking about our need as ministers to be needed and why this led to naivety. As I did, I noticed some jaws dropping and a fit of nervous coughs. I finished and one by one the group confessed that he had sold them the same pup. Many in their congregations were still praying for him! Later, I came to realise that there are people who are travelling not just Australia, but indeed the world on the gift of their gab and nerve. Whilst it is never pleasant to be badly fooled and ripped off, this experience did teach me a valuable lesson. What I gave away was only money. It was not the end of the world.

To become totally cynical, untrusting and hardbitten would be a much higher price to pay than accepting that the point of caring is to risk being ripped off. I believe that one can show charity and break the cycle of despair. Trust is more important than risking the rejection of those in genuine need. In any event, do not more honest, talented raconteurs do the same in earning a crust?

Sunday night live in St Kilda

⌁

In St Kilda, forty-two per cent of people live alone, whereas Melbourne's average is twenty-four per cent. Sunday evenings are often the loneliest times in the week. All the day-visitors who shop in the Esplanade markets and indulge in coffee and cake have driven back home to the suburbs. The routine of the working week has not yet come. Families of all configurations are sitting in their homes and flats tuned to *Sixty Minutes* or the movie of the week.

We were surprised on arrival to find that, like most everything else, the local churches were also closed. St Kilda Baptist had doggedly decided to keep an evening service going. For most of the 1970s only a handful of the faithful would gather to hear lay preachers take the services, reflecting the tenacity of this small remnant of believers. The Church of Christ in the same street had closed down completely in 1979. The local Uniting Church did not have an evening service. Even the Salvation Army Citadel had closed down, although their crisis centre in Grey Street continued to do significant work. But there was nowhere lonely people could just go, hear a message with some sort of hope, have a comforting cup of tea and somehow know that they were worthwhile.

So the doors remained open on Sundays and a steady stream of street people came out of the woodwork. The cup of tea or coffee and biscuits were the main attraction, but people generally knew that their 'payment' involved sitting through as much of the service as they could sustain before nicotine craving demanded a bolt for the door. This was the context we discovered in 1984. It actually inspired us.

Our older congregation had stuck with a three-hymn sandwich and an elevated pulpit to dignify the preached word.

Evenings were the traditional gospel service and sermons gushed with manly vigour and evangelistic zeal. An appeal for salvation was insistently offered by way of cajoling the street people and psychiatrically ill to repent. Soon the Eucharist (known in our circles as the Lord's Supper) was suspended because, in the view of our elderly congregants, it was suffering desecration. Left-field comments from the street people and a steady flow of traffic along the nicotine aisle out of the worship service had diminshed its reverence. Better to confine the privilege of communion to the more formal morning service where the 'saints' were more readily identifiable.

On arrival we immediately challenged this denial of the sacrament. It was reminiscent of older historical battles where, in the medieval church, he who controlled the sacrament controlled salvation. To our minds, the gospel was a free invitation to all peoples to the kingdom feast. The caution that this bread and wine is to nourish faith and should not be taken lightly is rightly given, but to deny the elements altogether is wrong.

At issue was a fundamental question of whether the grace of God is extended to all or whether church elders can play the role of a religious referee with a 'send-off' power. Should those who know the rules be able to punish others whose illness provokes apparently irreverent behaviour? Our belief was that the very brokenness of those suffering acute emotional and mental illnesses was encapsulated in the breaking of bread and the brokenness of Christ's body, which discloses God's love for all who suffer.

We had come to St Kilda because we knew that the gospel as presented in our Western evangelical ways was capable of building big churches in the Bible-belt areas, such as Blackburn, where we had both grown up, but our question revolved around its effectiveness to touch lives in regions beyond middle-class settings.

This is a question as ancient as the Bible. Israelites doubted that their God was able to hear their prayers in a foreign place like Babylon. They were no longer on God's turf; surely their prayers were rendered mute and dumb in a strange place? Arrogant though it sounds, our study of the gospels suggested that the middle-class church did not necessarily know much about Jesus of Nazareth. His inclusivity and scandalous friendships with social outcasts was an offence to normal notions of decorum. It was in the schizophrenic and psychotic that we discovered that the friendship of Jesus is for all. The good news of a loving, transforming presence in a callous world is for everyone, not just the beautiful who have capped teeth and professional careers. It is for all of humanity. Communion as an open table symbolises this conviction.

I remember one Sunday night cringing at the messages people had grown up hearing from the church. When the cup was being passed around, Kevin, who had just started coming, blurted out, 'Can I take communion? I am a bad man and have done time in prison.' He was encouraged to partake with the words that all of us fail God and ourselves and we all need the forgiveness that communion expresses.

Just at this point, one of the women we grew to know and love, an Aborigine called Eva, piped up. Turning to our ex-convict, she enquired, 'But wait on, love, have you had sex before marriage?'

He understandably looked a bit shocked and responded, 'Oh yeah, but what about everyone else here?' I noticed the rest of the congregation got rather itchy eyebrows, or at least they started rubbing them furiously, staring down at the floor. Most seemed relieved to treat this as a rhetorical question not demanding any further confessional candour. The cup was passed to Kevin and he took it and longingly drained it. He was so impressed that he exclaimed, 'Not a bad drop.' And for our diluted grape juice, that's saying something.

To some, this may read as a trivialisation of the most sacred meal. To us it was a penetration of the gospel that people named sins. For street people, the 'sins' they felt the church would pin on them were these very matters, such as time in prison and indulging in premarital sex. How could those with sexual peccadillos or criminal prior convictions be included in the communion of saints who were welcome at the Lord's table? Yet the old book depicted these very tainted people as the ones with whom Jesus shared table fellowship.

Table fellowship in Semitic culture was no casual business lunch where you settled a deal and moved on. It was a major social statement of profound proportions. You only ate with those whom you were willing to have publicly identified as your closest friends. Jesus mixed with the wrong crowd. Our middle-class training had taught us well that you are known by the friends you keep. Strangely enough, we were being liberated in St Kilda by a few modern-day examples of the friends of Jesus.

So communion became an open invitation, without a fencing rail and pastoral checks of communicants' prior convictions. I remember a Christian policeman coming to a packed evening service and showing signs of public discomfort throughout the service. He was stationed at St Kilda police station and rushed up to me after the service requesting that we speak privately. In an agitated tone he said, 'There is something you must know,' and then he discreetly pointed out five people that he knew had been charged or arrested over the previous weeks and related their various suspected offences.

I waited patiently for him to finish and politely thanked him for his concern. I simply asked him if he was pleased that they were in church. He looked shocked, then sheepish, and rather quickly excused himself. I have a hunch that Jesus would not blanch at such company.

We encouraged a sharing of personal struggles so the church might prayerfully support them at every communion service. Sometimes, this was like inviting an unguided missile attack.

One particular evening, a natural street poet was at church. He had suffered a massive breakdown at university and was later diagnosed as suffering from schizophrenia. Life became a series of transient boarding houses and seedy hotels, with annual admissions to hospital to stabilise him on different forms of medication. His pain and burning hope to be well was brilliantly verbalised in his poetry. That night in the sharing time, he shocked most by unblushingly asking for forgiveness because he had had a woman that week. Someone well intentioned but tactless unhelpfully chimed in, 'Well, at least it wasn't a man.' After the initial stunned silence at his frankness, people gathered around, laid hands on him in solidarity and love, and prayed for him.

The Letter of James in the New Testament exhorts us to confess our sins to one another. But in all my years of church attendance, I had never heard anyone take this that seriously. This act of self-exposure opened all of us to deeper levels of confession and truth-sharing. And once again, it was the street folk who led the way.

I started to see that this was why Jesus' famous Sermon on the Mount could blithely say, 'Blessed are the poor'. Many a mocking Marxist has torn apart this axiom with the critique that Jesus naively romanticised poverty, not knowing how dehumanising it was. But that night I thought, Yes, the poor *are* blessed because there is no mask needed, no image and respectable pretence to maintain.

Surely, this is why Jesus outrageously suggested that the prostitutes would enter the kingdom before the righteous. They were open to receive grace because they stood bare-headed and empty-handed without reputation and merit to commend themselves. Our wordy protective mechanisms had been pierced that night. Most of us could sermonise with theological sophistication about confessing sins to one another, but never risked its personal dimensions.

Class-based cultural diversity: the edges take shape

~

Our church motto was 'committed at the core and open at the edges'. In St Kilda, this required very open edges.

I had grown up with the maxim that cleanliness was next to godliness. I had heard it so many times when growing up that I assumed it must have been a quote from the Bible. In any event, it had seeped so powerfully into my subconscious that, during my first year in St Kilda, I simply could not credit that some of my congregation, the unsolicited and unkempt street people who could not get their personal hygiene together, were true disciples of Christ. They did not look like—and certainly did not smell like—the serious and responsible Christian citizens that I mentally associated with authentic Christianity. My cultural spectacles were so strongly focussed on the model Christian, one who curiously and coincidentally looked like me, that no amount of evidence of warm faith emanating from a smelly street person convinced me that this was a real Christian.

You can imagine my shock when I realised, with all the impact of a skydiver whose parachute had failed to open, that Jesus of Nazareth would have been an intensely smelly person. First-century Palestine was not blessed with abundant hot water; Jesus was an itinerant on the dusty road, without regular lodgings. If ever there was a street Messiah, it was him. Rapidly, I tried to adjust my cultural bearings to see with more biblical objectivity.

If twentieth-century hygiene was not a saint's stigma, what other marks had I got wrong? My inner agenda was utterly culture-bound. I aimed to change people to be like me. Whilst I had broadened considerably through exposure to other cultures overseas, I had never encountered the street culture before.

I had attended a private boys' secondary school and rubbed shoulders with a lot of sons of stockbrokers, lawyers, doctors and architects. I had gone through Monash law school with sons and daughters of stockbrokers, lawyers, doctors and architects. I had mixed with the same group, only on a much wider cultural palette, in Switzerland, but still they were articulate, tertiary-trained people. Poor people had been my legal clients as a lawyer, but I was firmly in control and my degrees hung intimidatingly on the wall behind me to remind them of my power and prestige.

It was not until my St Kilda days that it dawned on me how totally contained life is. Indeed, you see reality from where you sit. Now, some of my friends within the congregation were not just poor but often dishevelled, on the nose and sometimes incoherent from psychotic episodes. But, paradoxically to me, they were still people of faith and hope.

Part of my self-discovery was how a middle-class back-ground equips us to focus on the future. Much of life is organised around securing that future by working hard in school to get a good education and a well-paid job, and then working hard to save for a home deposit or for travel. Whatever the goal might be for middle-class people, it exists only in the future, and our culture disciplines us to sacrifice now in order to gain the future reward.

Street people, by contrast, are not futurists. They live almost entirely in the present. If they have money, instead of saving it, they throw a party, invite everyone, have a roaring good time and are impecunious again the next day. Living in the present is almost total. The really desperate live totally in the past and still try to settle deals for yesterday's debts and wrongs.

Now there is much to commend a futurist approach. It grants order and a planning that are great gifts, but the future goals are not necessarily morally superior to those of the present. Indeed, I could mount a solid biblical case that Jesus of Nazareth, who was accused of being a wine-bibber and party creature by his religious enemies, may well have thrown a party if he had any capital. He certainly had no house, or even the makings of a deposit, and he likened the dawning of God's new world to someone who would sell all and risk every asset for this kingdom—the celebratory festival of life.

A parable of the streets: a mother and daughter

⌁

Eva Briggs was the offspring of a rough whaler/sealer from Flinders Island near Tasmania and an Aboriginal mother. The sealers were bounty hunters beyond the law, more akin to pirates than colonial subjects. Folklore spun brutal stories of these sealers raping and pillaging defenceless Aborigines, whose life tenure was unpromising enough, thanks to the genocidal black hunts decreed by Governor Arthur.

The Briggs family drifted to the mainland and were protected on an Aboriginal reservation at Healesville. In 1961, at the tender age of nineteen, Eva fell pregnant to a sailor who blew into her life—and out again just as quickly. She had been raised in the Open Door Home for Girls. Indeed she was one of the Stolen Generation, a term I only came to understand years later thanks to the Human Rights and Equal Opportunity 'Bringing Them Home' Report. The stern warnings and Christian training did not prevent her pregnancy, such was her heart hunger for love.

Eva was persuaded to adopt the baby out at birth. She agreed with a heavy, aching heart. The consolation that she clung to as a sedation for the pain of separation within hours of birth was that her daughter had been adopted into a good Christian family.

Eva suffered from manic depression. Her broad brown face was marked by a burn that disfigured one complete side. Yet the compelling feature of Eva's face was not the scar, but her enormous smile. Since she was a regular member of my congregation, I began my pastoral ministry by visiting her at the Regal Hotel in Fitzroy Street. She was living with a man with drug-induced schizophrenia whose father was a university professor.

I recall knocking on the door of her room, number 108, and the first words Eva said to me left me pastorally winded. 'Come in, pastor; it is so good to see you. There's no fornication in this room, pastor. We are too tired for it, aren't we?' she said with a sincere nod at her partner. I did not laugh or cry, but shook my head in amazement at how un-textbooklike this ministry was likely to be. Her next topic was the one it would always be: should she have adopted her daughter out at birth? The guilt mixed with deep love always led her to doubt the wisdom of that decision.

In church, Eva was a genius at bringing us back to earth and grounding our worship and teaching in the reality of St Kilda. She never failed to interrupt the service with a reminder to me: 'Don't forget to pass around the offering plate, love.' Oft times that was the very item in the service that I did forget but for Eva's ministrations. She played the piano by ear—a rare gift cultivated in the Christian orphanage.

One evening service, we had invited a former professor of theology from our old college in Switzerland to speak. I warned him that there could be some feisty audience participation. He looked puzzled and fearful. I explained that you rarely got through a service uninterrupted because no-one had ever convincingly explained the church rule to the street people—that only those with theological degrees could preach and the congregation had no participatory role other than singing and nodding silent assent to the message. It was their service, they participated freely and fully, and no argument to the contrary was going to change that.

As the preliminaries unfurled, I realised that we were in for a rocky ride. Eva was in fine form as usual and pleaded with the crowd to help the wheat farmers who were suffering drought by only buying Australian-made Tip Top bread. She added, 'Please do not eat any foreign rubbish like Bornhoffen bread.' I inwardly grimaced and glanced sideways at our guest preacher, a German theologian. To my relief, he was not the least bit offended and seemed bright-eyed, nodding his head with unusual vigour. He leant over to me and said in a low voice with great respect, 'I'm impressed that she knows about Bonhoeffer!' (Bonhoeffer was a German theologian.) I realised with a sinking heart that he and Eva were not going to quite connect.

He got up and started to preach a solid and erudite sermon. Eva listened patiently enough for the first ten minutes, but then her concentration lapsed and she noticed some glazed eyes and indifferent looks around her, so tried a spot of her own spontaneous narrative theology. She interrupted him in full flight, saying, 'I've got a question.' Our guest looked relaxed enough because anyone who knew the German theologian Bonhoeffer's writing had to be on his wavelength. She said, 'We had a lovely young German doing the garden for us down at the Regal Hotel, but he has disappeared. Do you know where he has gone?'

Now that did throw our guest and his terrified look suggested he was out of his depth. After a long silence, he replied with a disarming push of pragmatism, 'Perhaps he went back to Germany.' Eva let out a disbelieving sigh and said, 'Oh no, he was much too young for that.' Others in the congregation conjured up visions of her fears of the Nazis still in power.

Eva was the local Mother Teresa. She included everyone in her circle of friends and displayed fastidious compassion for those who were ill or distressed. A natural networker, her small, smoke-filled room at the Regal was constantly choked with lonely and knocked-about St Kilda drifters.

I remember watching the parable of the widow's mite enacted by her, with me, a humble observer, melding into the background and marvelling at her sacrificial generosity. She was holding court in her bedroom, the windows as always securely fastened and the stale, smoky air suffocatingly close. But the camaraderie was as refreshing as pure oxygen. People were swapping stories of misfortune, with Eva pronouncing her matriarchal blessing: 'Never mind, love, you're safe here.'

In stumbled a burly, breathless guy with a story of woe about being rolled and then ripped off down the street. He had no chance of making it to pension day. Without hesitation, Eva rose to go over to her drawers and take out a twenty-dollar note: 'Here, love, take this.' His eyes glistened with unfeigned gratitude, and with stuttering thanks he rushed out. I asked Eva how much she had left until pension day and she said that was her last penny, but Jesus would want her to help others first.

I quietly rejoiced at her freedom to give all she had away. How many of us who have read and even preached on Jesus' invitation in the gospel to sell all and come and follow him have spiritualised it because it hardly constitutes sound advice in an economic-rationalist world? Here was someone free enough to obey.

Eva died on Melbourne Show day in 1992 at the age of fifty-three. She had a heart attack in her stomping ground of Fitzroy Street. We discovered upon her death that Eva had been as much at home with the local Catholics as she had with us Baptists. She had worshipped there too, and had even been baptised by them. So her funeral was a wonderful joining of the two traditions, as well as the diverse strands of her life. Street people, Koories and churchy-types crammed into the church sanctuary and paid their respects to a true lady whose passing they grieved.

Our worlds would perhaps have never touched so intimately but for Eva. But there was one significant loose end, the untied strand that meant the most to Eva. One Sunday, not long after her funeral, I was preaching at our church and two newcomers introduced themselves as visitors for the evening from a bayside Baptist church. At the conclusion of the service and after the mandatory coffee and chat, they were still there and obviously waiting for me. They asked to talk privately. A dark-haired, brown-eyed woman blurted out with tears rolling down her face that her name was Lyn and she had just found a few days ago that her natural mother was Eva. A family friend who knew the story had informed her adoptive mother that her natural mother was dead.

I felt blown away with joy and grief. Eva's beloved daughter was found, but found too late for either to ever know the other. She had Eva's same striking musical gifts, not part of her adoptive parents' gifts, and was a happily married mother of three and a piano teacher.

She had a thirst to discover all she could and fill the yawning curiosity and emptiness. I took her to the seedy Regal Hotel, Eva's last home, and watched her culture shock as she absorbed the poverty and smelt the musty air that carried a stale edge of urine. She met many of Eva's shabbily dressed friends. I saw disbelief mirrored in her eyes and vividly remembered my own culture shock the first time I had visited Eva. How hidden away this world is from the middle class.

But Lyn also discovered the authenticity of her natural mother's life. The contradictory data were as compelling as the culture shock. Everywhere people greeted Eva's daughter with joy and celebration. Their love for Eva captured your attention and held it against your will. Her mother was a remarkable and special person. Eva's friends were equally spontaneous, accepting people and intentionally deaf to the whisper that Eva's daughter was born on the wrong side of the marmalade toast.

We had the privilege of Lyn coming to church and sharing her journey of fear and fascination. The fear was the loss of a mother she had planned to meet but left too late, and also of the huge distance she must travel to understand her Aboriginality. The fascination was the joyous recognition that she had been deeply loved, prayed for and proudly owned by this unknown mother who had been a fountain of love to so many lost and unlovely people. That morning in church, there was hardly a dry eye as we who had known Eva felt privileged to complete the circle of love broken but not destroyed by Eva's death.

The conviction that death is not the final word allows us to grieve and then rediscover hope. A new beginning, energised by Eva's unconditional acceptance, has triggered for some a wave of grace in our hearts. Eva's consolation that her daughter had gone to a Christian family had been honoured, and Lyn shared the faith her mother had treasured.

An open pulpit

One of our firmest discoveries was the importance of an open pulpit, particularly one open to women and lay ministry. Women preachers seem more able to tell the congregation who they are, whereas male preachers tend to tell them what to do.

The long church tradition of ordaining only men ceased in our denomination in the mid-seventies. Despite this, only a handful of women have been ordained. Without risk of contradiction, I think that the most appreciated preachers in our pulpit have been women. They are earthy and honest enough to function like the preacher in one of Henry Lawson's famous stories. The outback preacher did not tell his hearers battling flood and bushfire that things would be better if they trusted God. He told them that things might endure even as now, but life was still meaningful and there is beauty in the suffering.

That message transforms the ordinary. It has been this sort of preaching that has reminded us that God inhabits the natural recesses of life as much as the supernatural and that we can find him in our daily experiences.

Caring: programs or community?

At first, we exhibited a Pavlov's-dog response to the needs we discovered in St Kilda. Our reflex reaction to the entrenched, seemingly insuperable problems was to devise a program. Now programs are very necessary as a way of addressing solutions and structuring existence, but they are rarely a substitute for a listening ear, an accepting hug or a comforting presence through the long, dark night of pain.

It is a feature of modern society that we have been convincingly creative in devising welfare bureaucracies to soften the burden of poverty or misfortune. But as many a social commentator has wryly observed, the bureaucracies are more adept at securing the welfare of bureaucrats and social workers than the welfare of the poor. Many a brilliant new welfare program carries a venomous sting in the tail of a costly and excessive professionalism to accompany the glossy new promises for the poor. Paradoxically, many of the same programs produce the very opposite effect to that which is intended. How often has the burst of additional funding only created a new high priesthood of social expertise who have succeeded in exchanging one form of dependency for a new one? In its wake is left the institutionalising of the experts' indispensability.

It is a fascinating realisation to see that the war on poverty in Australia may not have made the strides it boasts. Our

encounter with poverty in St Kilda suggested that, notwith-
standing the analysis and the political vows of overcoming child
poverty, the result has been to tread water. Whilst there is no
doubt that material poverty is less today, courtesy of a greater
community affluence than in the 1930s, it is arguable whether
life is better.

During the Depression, there was still that rather intangible
gift called community. The men in the street were not so
stressed by work-performance contracts that they were not
home soon after work to play cricket in the street with their
own kids and the kids of a deserted mother. A casserole would
still turn up on that deserted mother's doorstep. If a man
extinguished the pain by drinking too long at the local watering
hole, someone guided him home to his bed. Neighbourhood
relationships endured and, as in some country towns still today,
everyone related to each other, even the town drunk.

Privatisation has been a social process that extends beyond
public utilities. Its tentacles reach right into our families and
communities and make relationship less significant. Despite
greater communication systems in the mobile telephone, fax
and car, people are visiting friends less and spending fewer
hours with their families than in previous generations. We build
our homes in neighbourhoods without the intention of throwing the doors open to the life of the street. In place of a friendly
swinging gate, we place a speaker box, button and locked gate
to monitor entry. Little is left to spontaneity and neighbourliness. Our friends may live on the other side of the city and
our social lives revolve around clubs, whether sporting, religious
or cultural, that bar entry to those not like us.

The council next to St Kilda (another inner-city area) tried
to convince applicants who sought permission to build huge
front fences to desist because it damaged neighbourhood and

lessened security. They ran an education program to explain how this excluded community and did not enhance safety. It was all to no avail. These new residents wanted a house like grandmother's, with wide windows and a big verandah, but they did not want grandma's open home and its neighbourliness.

Caring: hospitality or charity?

'Marj' was a middle-aged Australian who lived a few doors up. It was hard to understand how such a sane, loving mother, whose daughter was unusual in the street because she went to a private school, would drop off the pier into a sea of insanity. As we came to understand mental illness, we realised how it is no respecter of persons, and the most capable, charming humans are its victims.

When Marj spiralled into sickness, she would still express herself with clarity and conviction about men who were hunting her and how we must not trust her husband who was in league with them. Confidentialities that were shared explicitly with the request that I must not tell others made it awkward. A number of times Marj would arrive in her nightie, breathless and pleading for a safe bed to escape pursuit. We would make up a bed for her in the kitchen as we had no spare rooms.

I remember the surprised looks on the faces of our guests one evening as Marj arrived, unpacked a lucid and terrifying story, and then relatively calmly took an aspirin and went to bed in the kitchen. Sometimes she would need hospitalisation, but often the psychotic episode would pass with the night.

The hospitality of those who are poor is often so determined as to invite trouble. 'Mary' was a woman in prostitution we worked with until her heroin addiction claimed her life in an overdose. Her sex work was driven by the needle, nonetheless she maintained a range of loyal friendships. I regularly popped in for afternoon tea.

Once I had some others visiting St Kilda and asked her if they could also come by and say hello. She was more than happy to entertain us with a lavish spread of chocolate Tim Tams in her bedsit. I remember my friends choking on their mouthful when Mary deflected their thanks with an explanation that she had specially gone down to the supermarket to pinch the biscuits. Hospitality was a higher priority than honesty.

The world of professional competence and control really has no place for the poor; it can manage charity, but not compassion or solidarity. But even charity for psychiatrically ill and homeless marginal people is accommodated to the managerial norms of social control, and rarely to the needs of people. We discovered that so many psychiatrically ill people desired not another drop-in centre providing a cup of tea made by paid professional staff, but a cup of tea freely offered in a family home. The programmatic response could never disguise, however professionally delivered, the clinical distance of the carer from the object of care. And it is hard to swallow the humiliation of knowing that you are an object of care.

We started to feel that the very act of compassion that invited the poor into the mainstream of our lives was subversive. The dominant welfare culture stills the groans and anaesthetises the pain and then goes on with business as usual. Sadly, the notion of human compassion and justice is rarely the first consideration in establishing a society.

Our religious vision taught us that Jesus walked on both sides of the street. His style was not one of dispensing 'you beaut' social welfare programs. He engaged in relational encounters that set people free because they did not start out with an intention to squeeze them into a program that would keep them out of sight and out of mind of the dominant consumer culture. He physically touched the most hideously marginalised in Palestine, the lepers, whose contagion was feared and whose colony was so despised. If lepers could be normalised by such love, then that is the vision for a truly human society. Jesus had friends, not clients.

Of course, part of the irony of well-intentioned programs lies in the reality that those who are paid generously to consult have little contact with or experience of the poverty that they are addressing. (I think the word 'consultant' should be struck from the vocabulary because it masks the fake expertise of often highly paid, incompetent, theoretical advisors.)

I was asked in an interview in the Melbourne *Age* in June 1994 what I thought of our State Government treasurer admitting he knew no poor people. I was stunned at this admission and replied that those who targeted welfare programs and guided our governmental spending must not be allowed to pontificate on meeting people's needs when they are not sufficiently bothered to even meet the people themselves. The word 'compassion' means *with passion*—with one's guts bursting with empathy for others. That is experienced only by looking into the eyes of those whose pain is deep. Planning programs without first stopping to hear the stories of struggle in poverty is passionless and produces distorted care.

Caring: companions or clients?

~

Funerals are one of the privileges of clergy. Australians increasingly are bypassing the church for weddings, but still turning to it in droves when it comes to funerals. At the end of life's day, there is something deeply comforting in the mystery of faith. Indeed, keeping religion out of the rites to say farewell to a life is nearly impossible.

I remember speaking at the funeral of a prominent communist union secretary who was married to a member of our wider family and being told beforehand that there was to be strictly nothing religious whatsoever. The music of the 'Internationale' led us into the memorial service. Various political and labour leaders spoke, including a strictly non-religious word from me. Then, to my amazement, the trade-union band struck up involuntarily a rendition of 'Amazing Grace' and weeping eyes and choked voices started heartily singing. Hope has a religious dimension and being a companion on the last journey with people when they die is where the most profound spiritual work is accomplished. And I find it happens within me as much as within the one making their final sojourn.

Funerals are often less well attended because employers are reluctant to allow the time to be lost. I think this is tragic, as honouring a life and honouring that part of ourselves that we are laying to rest is spiritually significant. It is a part of ourselves because, with every death of someone we know, something unique in us dies, as no-one else can evoke the same feelings or emotions as the one who has died. Christian funerals are the occasion to state that death is not extinguishing someone's lamp, but just putting it out because the dawn has broken for that person.

I am impressed with the seriousness and commitment of older people who attend funerals. They are a generation that still come from stable communities with continuity of traditions, where strong ties have created respect for more than just close friends. The loss of these communities in the fast-flowing transience of life is vividly seen at funerals. Where networks are weak through modern mobility, fewer turn up to remember.

Visitors to our church were profoundly struck by its inclusivity, for the most life-changing explosions are those that lift the veil of prejudice and allow the person to be seen. There was Annette who, though over fifty, had a mental age of a five-year-old and wore a tea cosy as her favourite head covering to church in winter. Annette's job was to take up the offering, which she loved to do. She had her own particular system that usually meant a few rows were missed and the 'takings' were down, but it was her job and it gave her great status. If a baby was in the congregation and the mother was trusting enough, as most had learned to be, Annette would walk up and down the main aisle nursing, oblivious to all else, particularly the preacher. Her childish delight was more eloquent than the sermon, echoing the apostle Paul's life-giving words: 'God has chosen that which is foolish in the world's eyes to confound the wise.'

Annette's usual companion in the task of taking up the offering was Bruce. He suffered a number of disabilities and stumbled rather than walked. He always sat in the front row and made a grand entrance, stumbling and lurching at a pace that caused visitors to catch their breath, thinking it must end in disaster. The regulars knew that somehow his timing to collapse only into his chair was impeccable. Bruce always carried a handbag, which would vary in size and colour each week. His ease with the congregation was such that no-one blushed at the pants at half-mast or the jolting manner in which his offering plate got thrust into your hands.

Katie was a twenty-year-old whose abiding love was her mice. Most of us enjoy private hobbies, but Katie saw no reason not to share hers with her church family. During the first service at which her pet rat appeared, popping its head curiously out of her blouse and running along her shoulder, there was a striking movement of the spirit. Pew-sitters who rarely participated spontaneously found their feet a-movin' as they sought safety from their rodent phobias in back rows.

Friends like Annette, Bruce and Katie can have caseworkers assigned to them when they become restive and socially difficult. But the deinstitutionalisation that gives them a chance of normalisation is inadequate. It places them in special accommodation centres that become an alternative institution out in the community. They continue to speak of their wardrobe as a locker and know that, despite their deepest hopes, they remain someone's client. Unashamed friendship is hungered after, as one would expect of anyone who desires companionship and not clientship.

As a response to the presence of these three in our midst, the church embarked on an ambitious program of buying and managing the special accommodation home where they lived. Though it cost a bomb—nearly one million dollars for both purchase and renovation to its former glory as a grand old two-storey St Kilda home—it now houses over sixteen people all like Bruce and Annette and Katie. It has been designed to give people their own bedroom, rather than squeezing four or five into undersized dormitories.

While the size still risks an institutional rather than a family feel, if we had not bought this dilapidated mansion, then further loss of housing stock and a further expulsion of St Kilda's psychiatric sufferers from an area that has good supports may have resulted. These people are often distinguished from many others who suffer this debilitating condition of psychiatric illnesses in that they have no-one else—no family or stable friends—to care for them. The aim is that the house be run not as a medical shelter program but as a home and a community to integrate their lives into ours and the local community.

We are positive about medicine but do not use the medical model. Too many people have seen medication used as a control mechanism to sedate and manage them. Sometimes it is necessary to protect others from too much shock. One of the occupants, a middle-aged woman, took to running down the main street completely naked. But our model aimed at a relational approach which recognised that anger and frustration did not always need to be bombed with drugs to be managed, but that the sufferer needed to be offered patience, friendship and understanding—costly in time, but much more healing. We letterboxed and visited all the neighbours within a half-kilometre radius to introduce ourselves. The idea was to explain that our residents might suffer from mental illness but they had the same hopes and fears as the rest of us. They wanted to be greeted in the street and contribute as they could. We hoped to overcome the caricatures of 'they're dangerous because they're different'. It worked wonderfully. One neighbour said a resident regularly urinated in her letterbox and she was too fearful to tell anyone. We acted quickly. Others realised they could ring us rather than the police.

The local neighbourhood

Our third child Martin arrived in January 1986. We named him after Martin Luther King Jnr, hoping he would capture a vision for justice like that great Baptist minister had done. But the name Martin means 'man of war', and we quickly discovered that he had arrived replete with the energy of an army. We realised our days in the two-bedroom flat next to the church were numbered. We were not sorry to move, as the steady flow of charity gold-seekers who found the church and then immediately moved to knock on our door was wearisome. Neither would we miss the drinkers from the Queens Arms who would be evicted at 1.00 am and then take up their revelry on our front fence.

Many a night, a post-closing-time drinking session would turn ugly and the foulest words followed by violent blows would fill our airwaves and float through our bedroom. It always gave us a helpless feeling, as they would be gone by the time the police came, and it was only a nuisance to the police when bigger events warranted their attention in St Kilda's twilight world. So our fast-track local education, inculcated by living diagonally opposite a working man's pub, finished when we bought a house in a nearby street.

The house, which we purchased at auction, was advertised as great potential for a renovator. We were certainly not in that category, but regrettably fitted the 'renovator's dream' price bracket. Its rundown state added enormous unsought stress and kept us busy for some time. However, despite the rubble of many years' worth of beer bottles, the former owner having been an old alcoholic, we did unearth some treasures, including some pristine 1940s editions of the *Australian Women's Weekly* from under the lino. We framed the front covers to hang on our walls and remind us of those renovation battles without money for proper tradesmen.

We also made our immediate neighbour's acquaintance, thanks to my extensive inexperience with tools. I was drilling some power sockets into a party-wall that separated our lounge room from the house next door. I was happily concentrating on the task when some furious pounding on our front door erupted and could be heard even above the noise I was making. Annoyed at the interruption, I turned the drill off and walked to the door. There was our neighbour, whom we had never met, rather good-humouredly saying, 'You can stop drilling now—you are right through into my lounge room.' This unorthodox beginning nevertheless led to a good relationship, especially once I plastered his wall back into shape.

There were two chilling remarks that greeted our arrival in our new street. The first was from a mountainous woman neighbour who couldn't hide her toothy smirk at the news that I was a clergyman. She recovered her wits enough to stop falling about with amusement and comment that this was good news, as the street could do with some cleaning up. The second comment came from a local policeman who candidly expressed disbelief that any responsible family would freely choose to buy in Marriott Street. The police paddywagon knew the route by automatic pilot, such were the number of distress calls, most of them assaults, that emanated from the two hundred metres of street that boasted our semi-detached house. That set us back because we knew the folklore that six months stationed at St Kilda was worth five years of police experience anywhere else. Was this street going to age us as quickly? I was only too soon to ruminate on how rapidly my criminal practice built up from our own street. It was an unintended aspect of bringing work home.

Our house was an Edwardian, single-fronted solid-brick, but virtually every window faced south, so it could be very dark, even on the brightest summer's day. It was one of only ten houses in the street. The streetscape was filled in with about twenty blocks of two- and three-storey flats with no garden or greenery and little parking. These flats had been thrown up in the 1960s when permits were lax and developers smelt easy money.

As the street held some of the cheapest flats to let in St Kilda, the most amazing array of humanity floated in and out. People were always moving as the turnover was necessary to maintain sanity. The street's visible signature was the moving van and, as these cost money, they were complemented by overloaded station-wagons, jalopies, and even wheelbarrows groaning with the irregular loads hauled up and down stairs and the short street. Couches, tables and junk always lay scattered over the nature strips and footpath, often just heaved out the nearest flat window.

One Sunday morning on walking home from church, Merridie discovered the nature strip opposite us covered for metres with bulky pieces of timber. They came, she was told, from a little old hermitic man on the third floor of the flats opposite who was moving out after twelve years. His obsession was hoarding bits of wood. By the time I got home, Merridie and the kids had collected boxloads of it, enough for many winter's log fires. Such surprises were common in the neighbourhood. With a few hundred people in the street living in such close proximity, we were plunged into an intense and vulnerable sea of relationships.

Living in this street directly exposed our children to the rawest underworld. Drunks were a common sight and discarded and dangerous syringes frequently lay on the footpath. The redlight area was only two hundred metres away, so used condoms were not uncommon.

The small park in our street was an open space for users and for people in all states of depression and manic episodes. Domestic violence was also common. Our first brush with television news was actually after an ugly screaming match in our street occurred early one Sunday morning. When Merridie came back later from church, all the commercial news cameras were outside our front fence and she was interviewed about what was being regarded as an abduction of a woman that morning. Merridie's version was less colourful than some of our neighbours' and it ended up being screened on the news that night, and proven accurate by police investigation. It was simply as Merridie had suspected a case of a recalcitrant eighteen-year-old drunken daughter being taken home with some force by her family from an all-night rage.

Besides the park in the street, another main meeting place to encounter some of our immediate neighbours was the Salvation Army's needle-exchange centre down the road. To prevent the spread of HIV (the virus that causes AIDS) from hurtling through the community via intravenous drug users, over 50 000 clean needles were being handed out to users each month. The tragic personal anguish associated with drugs was frequently evident in the neighbourhood.

Sometimes, the familiarity with the darker side of life fashioned in our children its own black humour. In 1991, when we were enjoying a family holiday during a three-month sabbatical I had in New Zealand a ten-year-old Kiwi friend was boasting that her relatives had been aristocrats who had come out from England. Claire patriotically rose to the challenge and said her ancestors were from England, too, but they had been sent out as condoms. We had to do a quick job explaining our 'convict' origins, or at least those we thought we might have had.

Opposite us in one of the tiny summer hot-boxes that passed for a flat was a single mother, 'Susan'. Over time, we discovered that she had lost her first child, a daughter, to welfare. She was zealously protective of her son 'John', but we noticed that after we had gained her trust she not only let John come and play, but let him stay for long hours that presumed on our goodwill. Susan was in a relationship with a nineteen-year-old who was an Australian model of Arnold Schwarzenegger. I remember thinking that his voice box was as big as my chest. He and Susan found the company of the pub and the competition of the billiards table more congenial than their tiny and messy flat.

John was older than our kids and desperate for attention. His second year at primary school saw him coming home to an empty flat and frequently bunking in at our place for dinner and even staying overnight. Mum would pop over at increasingly late evening hours and disingenuously scold John for wandering over when he should be home. The need to cover up for her absence and lack of cooking was sufficiently impressed on him to make him surreptitiously slink over and request some money to buy himself an evening meal of potato cakes. The kindly local publican gave him, a seven-year-old, bottle-stacking work to pay for his diet of potato cakes.

Susan was not amenable to any sensitive entreaties on our part that her mothering might adopt some alternative approaches. She was obsessed with her relationship breaking up and, as we soon discovered, her musclebound partner had inseminated her best friend in the street.

Meanwhile, John was losing any systematic pattern of parenting. We realised that this was a repeat cycle of neglect where Susan essentially could cope with the baby and infant stage, but not with responsibility thereafter. It is one thing to be a lawyer representing a distraught mother who is sure that officious government interferers are just projecting their own middle-class parenting values inappropriately onto them. It is another to be faced with the awful choice of reporting a child as being at risk to the State welfare authorities, knowing the shattering betrayal of trust that it will signify to the mother. However, one would have to suffer from acute glaucoma not to see that Susan was utterly failing in providing even the minimum levels of consistent care.

Sadly and surprisingly, she was not too upset—and perhaps even a tad relieved—when John was removed from her care. But it gave us little joy to watch John's grief. It reinforced the axiom that often the worst home is preferable to the best institution, as a sense of family belonging, so critical to identity, is smashed. We kept up with John. He took to running away from his various foster homes and ending up on our doorstep with unlikely stories of having been given permission to come.

Another family, a single mother and her son, lived in the flats and they seemed different from the start. Our kids brought home 'Mike', a boy who incessantly scurried around like an ant on a hot barbecue. He was likeable, but his hyperactivity suggested he was fragile. Soon, our children started to bring home stories that his mum was weird. They did not know why, but everyone in their gang of friends agreed she sure was different to their mums. I noticed she was different when we played football in the park and discovered she was punting the football ten metres further than me. Her large hands gave the game away. I realised to my shock that Mike's mum used to be Mike's dad. He had undergone a sex change and was now a woman. And the doctors had done a passable job—except for the hands.

Such is the rough honesty of the street that this dark secret soon became a tradeable commodity, with the older teenagers initiating our kids into the secret. Their confusion was small compared to the excruciating taunts that Mike had to endure. We determined to do all in our power to provide an accepting and protective safe place in our home for him to play.

Mike continued to live a pretty normal life, but with moments of great fear and defensiveness. His loyalty towards his mum was exemplary. But now and then there was still a descent into a *Lord of the Flies* scenario, as someone whose family was so different was maliciously turned on by the gang in the street. Despite all liberal anthropological protestations that children are blank sheets without a trace of malevolence and only learn unkind behaviour from adults, I can only cite our observation of Mike's treatment to say how devastatingly cruel children can be.

Transformers

In the early days we formed an after-school children's club called the Transformers. It was sheer hard work. The kids would arrive after school like unwound springs and bounce off the walls of the small dilapidated church hall. The cordial and bikkies we offered to settle them down only seemed to stoke them up. Often, their violence towards each other was flashpoint and unpredictable.

A family of three siblings were so violent and angry with anyone who got in their road that I decided to visit the home. I found it packed with 'hot' goods. Dad was a professional criminal and averted his eyes when he saw me in my lawyer's suit a month later at the local court. Another boy, who lived in our street was being expelled from primary school—which takes a lot of effort.

We hung in with the Transformers, often licking our bruised egos and musing that they were transforming us more than we were transforming them. Now, ten years later, that emotionally demanding work is paying off; some of them as young adults seek me out and remind me that it was the Transformers where they felt safe. Despite its chaos, it was a warm club in a bleak, often scary and violent world. A safe experience is often an isolated peak in many a child's flat emotional landscape and it had become, for a few of the Transformers, a treasured memory that life could be positive.

The diversity of and pressures on family life

We have had cause to view the current debate over the family from the underside of family life. The 'family' has become a political football. Conservatives stress their preferred definition of a heterosexual, two-parent family with children. Unfortunately, conservatives by definition always prefer to live in a world that no longer exists.

The progressive side is attuned to the vastly changed make-up of families, such as our neighbours in St Kilda, and wants to count them in. But in staggering from one new concept of family to another, it is hard to fix on any substance.

Our experience of the 'normal' two-parent family in Switzerland after the birth of our first child convinced us that it, too, is an inadequate life-support system. Not to have grandparents or other on-tap babysitters is never to escape. This we found almost too much and it introduced some of the worst stress we have experienced in our marriage.

The families in St Kilda that seemed most durable were those which blurred the line between nuclear and extended. A few of the cultures surrounding us had more fluid and extended models which appeared to make no distinctions between siblings and cousins, parents and uncles and aunts, treating them all as family. Parental authority was freely exercised by whichever adult was on duty. For some teachers and authorities, this drew untidy lines of responsibility. For our Prussian minds that valued order, it was too flexible, but we observed how wonderfully responsive to the chaos of life this community model was.

It is interesting how the norm becomes whatever is prevalent. Merridie overheard Claire telling a girlfriend that I was not her real father, but only a stepfather. Her real father, she said in a confidential tone, was an alcoholic and lived up in the mountains. Merridie was amazed and interrupted a surprised and embarrassed Claire with the demand, 'Why are you saying this?' She replied, rather crestfallen, that most of her friends had fathers who were alcoholics and lived in the mountains.

We understood why past ages had organised life around extended families with lavish helpings of uncles, aunts, older cousins, and the like. But economic progress announced the use-by date for this type of family grouping. The radical social shift known as the Industrial Revolution broke up rural family networks as jobs vanished on the farms and flourished in the cities. The industrial hunger for transportable labour to fuel the smoking factories necessitated a mobile workforce. Extended families were too cumbersome, too blunt and unfocussed a tool for the new industrial appetites.

A neat, new mobile model called the nuclear family was born. Our observation of the Asian families that hit St Kilda as their first stop in Australia was that there might be economic grounds for the extended family to make a comeback (language our managerial culture understands). They would pile into an impossibly small and cheap flat for their numbers and organise an around-the-clock shift of work and home care. Pooling their incomes, the first family would get a deposit and move out, followed by the next according to the collective formula, and leave old Aussies whistling in amazement and contempt that these boat people could take up their part of the Australian dream way ahead of them.

In our local pubs, I met many a whingeing Australian crying into his beer and moaning about 'the chinks' that were ripping off their country. The extended family, or pragmatic communitarianism, was the clue to their success. This process was so striking that we realised that the Asian families not making it out of St Kilda were often the really depressed ones, or were those who bought back into the smart renovated houses as the newly gentrified class.

I felt at the time that the major political parties exhibited a dreary sameness in their shared myopia to the family. The ever-ascending pressures of their economic agenda were placing an ever greater pressure on families. In an economic-rationalist world (a worldview enthusiastically embraced by both sides of politics), the catchcry is perform or be punished. Now, there is truth in the need to compete with the rest of the world, but such catchcries are a selective presentation of it. Like all ideology, there are parts edited out and those parts are the communities and families who need to be factored in to moderate the grand plans for efficiency.

Both sides of politics have little inkling of the destructive pressures unleashed by economic-rationalist policies on families of all shapes and composition. I copped some flak for saying publicly that such policies were poisoning families. Anyone who dares criticise the collusive pact of what the economic future must be is caricatured as a loony Luddite. But the industrial-relations climate that pushed people out of any job security into performance contracts has ratcheted up the tension of work performance but failed to see the tension spilling over into family life. Husbands and wives who must both work to realise the Aussie dream of home ownership have internalised the message that if they fail to perform, then there are plenty of people out there who will tender for their jobs. Great for economic efficiency—but at what toll on the family?

It is not unusual that after a stressful day at work we come home tired to last night's dishes and are greeted by ratty kids demanding our attention. Our emotional exhaustion is not alleviated by the time-savers like dishwashers and microwaves as we feel bereft of quality time. This often focusses frustration on both our partners and our children. The kids seem wilfully oblivious to our stress and the more we ignore their attention-seeking antics, the more determined they become to get right up our noses. Partners find they are spending their worst-quality time together at home, and their most productive and most in-control times at work apart. Work claims the choicest portion, leaving the spent ends for the trifling matters of raising offspring and nurturing relationships. Little wonder marriages and families implode.

In the past, we recognised that maintaining a home with its child-rearing duties and maintaining an income-earning job were two full-time occupations. To straddle two income-earning jobs and maintain the home, we need to either retrieve domestic servants or to enlist extended voluntary supports. Domestic help is a boom industry (servants are back in) and grandparents are discovering that early retirement is a hidden minefield, as they are recruited to revisit exhausting parenting duties. We must find flexible working patterns to make work serve our families instead of families serving rapacious employers who want their pound of flesh.

Hugh McKay, in *Reinventing Australia*, describes families as living with the Last Straw Syndrome. One more stress may be enough to make us snap and want out. Little wonder also that the video or computer game becomes the babysitter and the dialogue partner for our kids. In a fast-firing economic world of the mythic 'level playing field', there is only so much psychic energy in us, and serious parenting receives the fag end. We have observed parents in St Kilda dolefully handing out caches of cash each weekend and saying to their teenagers, 'Take your adolescent chaos anywhere away from home and entertain yourself. I simply cannot cope with you any more.'

If these realities sap the energies of the 'ideal' two-parent family, they have enervated the life forces of the single-parent family. It has always been a battle to hold it together emotionally. Something of parental desperation is reflected in the epidemic of attention deficit disorder, with so many parents convinced that their children can be medically treated for what is commonly a social, not a medical, problem.

Commitment to a multicultural neighbourhood
⟶

Part of our street was an informally assembled United Nations. My background in Blackburn could not be more different than that of my kids. There, the only foreign-sounding name we knew was the football star, Ron Barassi. In Marriott Street, it was Indian, Vietnamese, Cambodian, Thai, Sri Lankan, black American, and so many more cultural backgrounds, that constituted their play friends.

The family to whom the children grew closest were Cambodians. The eldest three children were born in Thai refugee camps after their parents escaped Pol Pot's holocaust. The youngest, a daughter, was born upon arrival in Australia and was spontaneously named after the midwife who helped deliver her. The family came to Sunday school with our children each week at the church and their once-a-year trip to the Buddhist Temple found our kids reciprocating the religious experience. It was fascinating to hear earnest table talk between them as to who was stronger—Jesus or Buddha.

Our children had been inducted into the Father Christmas fiction, as we had been by our parents. So they were accustomed to waking up to many delightful presents on Christmas morning and believing that a North Polar, benign, sleigh-drawn visitor had mysteriously spread his favours during the night. One Christmas they excitedly rushed around to their Cambodian friends' flat only to discover that this kind figure had carelessly and thoughtlessly failed to show up. Upon their return home, their confused and crestfallen faces warned us that this fiction had a short shelf-life in St Kilda.

We started to discover the joys of sharing the Christmas spirit with our multinational and multireligious neighbours. Perhaps the most memorable Christmas Eve of all for us was in 1992 when, with Nepalese Hindus, Cambodian Buddhists and Indian Sikhs, we sat together in our lounge as the children sang us carols.

The father of our children's Cambodian friends had little English and, though I managed to secure him a job in 1990, bad economic times saw him, along with a large segment of the workforce, retrenched within six months of starting the job. He managed in that time to save and buy himself a car—a very important symbol of having made it, we discovered. After a few months of unemployment, he scored some seasonal work fruit-picking up in the northern part of the state. Coming from a peasant farming background, he was quite inexperienced on wet country roads and tragically spun out of control on a sharp bend, smashing into a tree and dying instantly. His 34-year-old widow saw the mangled car on the 5.00 pm news service before the police had relayed to her the tragic information. Her daughter came running down to our place screaming hysterically, and so Merridie raced up and was there as the police came.

It was the longest two-hour drive of my life to take this woman up to the country town mortuary to identify her husband's body. The coldness and unforgiving finality of death was overwhelming. To have survived the Khmer Rouge killing fields and listless years waiting in a Thai refugee camp only to perish on Australian roads at thirty-nine years of age felt absurd and obscene.

I conducted the funeral with five Buddhist priests. The body lay in a simple open coffin and my children, though only nine, seven and five years of age, touched the body with their grieving friends. It seemed very natural to them and enabled them to accept the cold reality of death. I realised that I had not seen a body until I was in my mid-twenties and then only as a discreet and distant 'viewer'. Here were my children brushing his cold hands and putting incense sticks around the coffin—and all this whilst the funeral was taking place.

I also noticed the very different sense of pastoral care. The Buddhist priests were not allowed to so much as even physically touch a woman, so there was no personal contact with the widow. Their ministrations were purely spiritual. As his body was buried with Buddhist incantations in the Methodist section of the cemetery, I wondered what the Wesleyan Anglo forbears in the neighbouring graves would have made of it all.

An Egyptian family in the street had come out to Australia on the pretext of a visitor's visa and then sought to stay, claiming that as Christians they were persecuted in a predominantly Muslim country. I acted for them legally in a forlorn case that never had sufficient evidence to satisfy our immigration sleuths. Their flat was literally littered with paper and dirt and the subtle loan of a vacuum cleaner was to no avail. They permitted their children to enjoy freehand painting on the flat walls. In our inexperience, we never quite determined whether this was a cultural issue or sheer indiscipline and wilfulness. But the fear and helplessness of those young children's big brown eyes when their parents hysterically cried at the arrival of the federal police to deport them still haunts me.

We found a flat for a wonderful Indian family who worked in community development with slum-dwellers in India and who had come out to study theology. Unfortunately, their kitchen window overlooked a balcony in the next block which the brazen female occupants used for their nude sunbathing. For members of a discreet culture that censored a passionate kiss in public movies, this was a strong and heady drop of Western culture. We took them shopping at the supermarket and they were like a kangaroo caught in a shooter's spotlight.

It was a deep culture shock to have such an overwhelming range of choice.

They kept asking with genuine bewilderment why there were not only different types of breakfast foods, but even the same type with different brands. Such duplication was beyond comprehension. Have you ever tried to explain to someone from the Third World, where poverty is appalling, why Australians find it so socially liberating to have a range of consumer choice? Thanks to their mystification, I gained a flash of insight into the madness of our consumer capitalism.

I started to understand that the new Cartesian truth was not 'I think therefore I am', but 'I shop therefore I am'. How many times are we given the message that, if we are anxious, stressed or just need a pick-up, there is a marvellous antidote: shop. Shop until you drop and feel the joy. This is curious given that the dilemma most of us face every Christmas is what to buy for loved ones and friends who already have everything. Instead of acting morally and buying them nothing in order to give the money to people in absolute need, we buy our loved ones something they don't have from the whole range of products that come onto the market. This mindlessly 'solves' our Christmas dilemma but in truth they do not need these things.

I could not but marvel at the religious dimensions that were infiltrating our consumerism. The architecture of our shopping malls is often framed with magnificent arches and even stained-glass and leadlight windows. To enter the cavernous department store is to enter a modern secular temple. Muzak has replaced the pipe organ; it soothes the troubled spirit in search of that mystical or spiritual breakthrough known as finding a 'bargain'. The counter could easily be a substitute communion table laden with life-giving elements, and the shop

assistant a secular priest extending the Eucharistic invitation—
come and touch, taste and handle.

If we commune by trying on the wares and nourishing our
spirit, we can expect a warm blessing: 'You look fantastic; you
will be so happy with this.' The message is true, at least
momentarily. We leave with the syrupy muzak still wafting and
the benedictional blessing ringing in our ears: 'Have a nice day.
You really scored a bargain.'

Most parents live with constant internal pressures to buy
their children the faddish clothing or toys peddled by advertising traffickers. They are irresistible because their idols like The
Spice Girls and soap stars offer their 'friendship' with the
product. It provokes a psychic nausea to see the absence of real
heroes—and their replacement with airhead media creations
who fill magazines like *Dolly*. Advertising is like the ancient
Aboriginal practice of throwing the leaves of the corkwood tree
into the waterhole and stupefying the fish by the release of its
medicinal properties. The fish float to the top, making for an
easy catch. We consumers, too, are stupefied by the promises
of pleasure in the glittering goodies and are an easy marketing
catch.

Of course, it is not the product itself, but the wrapping of
the product in emotional values that makes the sale. One beer
advertisement shows a father and son on an outback verandah
talking intimately. The hunger in most men for intimacy in
their relationships with their fathers is so strong that it ensures
a powerful identification with the beer that effects this miracle.
Most men want to share freely with their fathers, but are ashamed
to speak of the feelings within. They ring home and when he
answers he just grunts, 'Hello son, I'll get your mother.' In a
world where the 'father hunger' is so poignant, a brand of beer
that promises such a relationship is a sure winner.

Commitment to the local community

～

Many days we felt trapped because we had next to no backyard and Merridie's childhood on four acres of cherry orchard replete with a tennis court teased us with spatial memories. The park in the street was a welcome outlet for energy but we felt anxious about the children going there alone. It provided the venue for the street to mix, to play games, and even have the odd barbecue or picnic. But it could also be a place where unknown adults would sit and watch. We knew there was always a need to be protective, both of our own and others' children.

Oft times, caring people have lectured us that our lifestyle is for celibate priests and missionary adventurers. When we heard our daughter saying how nice it is to play in the park at Blackburn because there are no syringes or condoms, we reflexly glance from the blow. Singles unfettered by marriage and unburdened with children can take the risks of living on the edge of the danger zones. There is no doubt that a special calling exists for those people.

Naturally, it is entirely possible to live a comfortable and quite protected existence in St Kilda if you rule home out of bounds to any 'undesirables'. Many do just that. But as the home is the cradle of community, that would rule out so many possibilities for transformation of those excluded from the healing acceptance of family. The openness to brokenness and absorbing the pain of marginalised people must be brought into the mainstream.

At present, we have little more than a vision of subcultural existence that leaves everyone isolated in their social ghetto and erects a type of social apartheid. The Church must find its mission in the midst of marginalised communities and share its life fully. Too often, it sounds like the exuberant coach shouting instructions about how to play the game from the safety of the boundary line.

We knew, nonetheless, how fragile we were and our confidence only grew when other families moved in to join us in this vision. Many of these others who came to the church began to move into neighbouring streets and the shape of community evolved. In fact, so many others were doing just that that some estate agents assumed our lifestyle was similar to the Jewish pattern of having to live within walking distance of our Baptist synagogue. One commented to me that our area was becoming known as the Baptist sector—perhaps even a ghetto to the more suspicious.

However, this commitment to the St Kilda community was not based on it being a typical middle-class suburb. St Kilda is a suburb of rich and poor classes living side by side. Middle-class families are in short supply simply because the housing stock is too expensive. This is a surprise in a country that has been described enviously by an American commentator as having the biggest middle class in the world. A positional good is a scarce resource which cannot be easily replicated and a home in a beach location six kilometres from the city centre is just that. So the wider Protestant Church, which has long had a mortgage on middle-class family ministry with its Sunday schools, youth groups and respectable rhythm of religious worship, has struggled to be relevant to either rich or poor.

Protestant churches in St Kilda have dramatically shrunk and some have withered altogether on the religious vine. The Salvation Army congregation has died, sold up and moved its worshipping community out. They still have a frontier social, feeding and housing program, but now Ukranian Orthodox believers chant and swing their incense in the Salvo citadel intended for bonnets, tambourines and brass bands. Likewise, the Church of Christ sold its only church to a caryard and looked for softer ecclesiological climes. St Kilda's multicultural world was proving arid ground for a religion associated with Anglo-Saxon Protestantism. Catholics are proving a much more resilient Church and have actually grown through migration, particularly with the large Polish waves.

The WASP population that was living in St Kilda was not of the churchgoing strain. Strangely, it had developed a sophisticated immunity to the religious virus. Mainly yuppies, they found home renovation, theatre, restaurants, and living within spitting distance of cafes that could serve a cappuccino at 3.00 am all adequately met their needs. Often progressive in political attitudes and radical in social tolerance, the institutional Church looked to this group like something belonging to the *ancien régime*, a *passé* reactionary era. A rundown Baptist church that was situated in the midst of this world was not going to go down well.

So when we issued an invitation to some friends to begin a journey into community with us, it was to be more than just another church; it was an alternative lifestyle. It was a considerable risk as we had no money, no set plans, and only a vague hope that community promised the fragile prospect of fulfilling some shared dreams. We read the stories of other communities and saw that most raised expectations and hopes that they simply could not meet. Worse still, many ended up with more than a few disappointed people, and with angry and badly hurt people who feared to dream and be let down again.

It is an inexorable rule that dreams which anticipate so much also wreak the most havoc if they go wrong. This fear almost provoked a stillbirth for us. Asking individuals and families who are in St Kilda to join you is one matter. Calling families ensconced in their safe suburbia to risk all and move to cramped, rented premises in a city eschewed by most as posing an unacceptable risk in raising their children is another. Those people we called were prepared to look beyond the horizon and many are still living in this area.

One of the initiatives that we started in 1987 was to open an opportunity shop in Carlisle Street. It was to fulfill dual aims of providing some much-needed finances to back up the diverse ministries and serving as a shop front where the locals could find friendship along with a few bargains. We found a rundown shop at very good rental near the library and it was quickly set up by a team of eager workers. Diane Wilson, in particular, was the energy in getting this project up and running and Christine Davey also did a stirling job of support over the years.

The opportunity shop received donations from virtually all over Melbourne and provided a healthy source of revenue. Over the seven years it ran, at least $80 000 went into the ministry. It also provided a great place for people to work and feel useful. Volunteers even came each week from Blackburn. My mother Anne was the chief organiser of these great 'doers'. The shop introduced them to some of the rawest sights in St Kilda. They got used to dealing with persistent barterers, thieves and addicts, as well as the most delightful people just wanting to have a chat.

'Nancy' was a local woman who volunteered to help. She was the best of workers and a cheerful, generous soul, but she wanted absolutely nothing to do with the church. She had been embittered by something too sad to even mention. Nancy added colour and life to the place. She was great with people and even though lung cancer was slowly killing her she never missed a day of her roster. Eventually, from her hospital bed in the last few weeks of her life, she allowed a few of the pastors to visit and to hear her painful story. Sadly, she refused to have a funeral and insisted on a pauper's burial, as she felt that this was all she was worth. But we were able to acknowledge her life and her contribution to our lives by a simple service, and a poem which has been published in her memory.

It was people such as Nancy whose life touched all of us and reminded us that every face tells a unique and precious story, and that in community we all have an invaluable contribution to make.

Commitment to the local church

⌣

Our theology taught us that locality is important. Just as the Bible could reveal the intimate interplay between place and personality and give us Jesus of Nazareth, Paul of Tarsus and Joseph of Arimathea, so we wanted to permit the environs to shape us and we them. We had observed how casually many churches treated their neighbourhoods as disposable transit zones. The sociology of the motor car seduced many churches to advertise for people from some distance away, removing them from any possible ecclesiological participation in their local communities. Christian parents, wringing their hands about drugs and peer-group influences, will travel any distance to join a church that has a large youth group. Many subtly hand over the faith nurture of their troubled adolescents to the youth leaders.

To the shame of most denominations, we have watched our church leaders holding up these fast-growing churches that feed off small local parishes as the success models. Opportunism and expediency, masquerading as church growth, are but a feeding frenzy on smaller parishes. The bigger churches grow through church transference, not through conversions. Many of them know even less than the small church they have unwittingly plundered about transforming their local communities and seeing people come to faith. These entrepreneurial attitudes have often cynically triumphed over earthy commitment to local institutions and local communities. When the biggest churches are drawing people from all over a city of more than three million and immersing them in hectic and disembodied church programs, those who are needed to drop anchor are in short supply.

Regrettably, the church which gave business and the corporate sector terms like pastoral care and mission statements has surrendered its birthright to total quality management ideology. Esau has forgotten his birthright. Now, it is fine to see the customer as sovereign when offering a service or a product. It is fine to treat staff as the richest resource and demonstrate pastoral care. But remember, it is all directed to profit. The rich resource is savagely shed if the bean counters' computers show a dip in profit. Pastoral care, then, has a hollow ring.

Churches exist for the business of teaching that the least are the greatest and the last shall be first. The management mentality has some useful things to teach churches, but they have stampeded in an unholy rush pushing churches to act like corporate bodies. They do know about brand and specialisation for worship and music styles and have mapped the religious market. Consequently, much of the church-growth literature is about unabashed management principles, purporting to teach Jesus' world-famous management techniques. The only fly in the ointment is that Jesus showed no concern for falling numbers, profits or growth, and was so preoccupied with the integrity and relational truth of the kingdom that he failed to open many successful branch offices.

Unfortunately, there are churches today who want to be like supermarkets in gigantic shopping towns, and not corner stores. The growing churches see that it is only the elderly and dwindling number of loyal locals who provide custom at the local store. Everyone else drives to shopping complexes where there is good parking, wide choice of shops with fast service, and entertainment in music, theatres and kids' shows to distract the children. There is little risk of interruption or recognition and little commitment to stores, because you are not known.

This is undoubtedly flowing with the trend, but what has that got to do with transforming lives and communities? Contrary to the spurious claims of church growth that point to their burgeoning numbers as the work of the Holy Spirit, this is a secular, not spiritual, trend. The religious variant of the amalgamation we see in such bodies as trade unions and business is the growth of super-churches by Christian members transferring from small, local church communities who have one pastor and cannot specialise with a team of youth, counselling and music ministers. In my view, many of these growing churches know far less about evangelism, discipleship and community than the smaller ones that they are closing down— even though they do know more about sociology and management techniques.

Churches need to think again. The computer age will almost certainly turn the home into the workplace, as a modem is all that is necessary to connect with the office. If workers are living their whole lives at home, then neighbourhoods with parks and friends and shops will become important again. So will local churches that take their neighbourhoods seriously. So selling off these local houses of worship for the massive super-church hangars is perhaps sociologically short-sighted as well as theologically suspect.

Commitment to the local school

In 1984 it came as no shock to discover that St Kilda Primary had been classified in the top ten disadvantaged schools in the whole state. Nice to be in the top ten of something. But the energetic principal had set about reversing that trend. He wrangled sponsorship from the local traders for school scholarships and found government funds for programs that the government didn't even remember existed. His vision and vigour was a tonic in an area accustomed to defeatist attitudes.

The school itself was avoided by some health-conscious parents. It is located on a triangular apex where two of Melbourne's busiest roads meet. Lead poisoning has been the calling card from cars that use St Kilda as a freeway transit zone to roar into work and back out to their leafy bayside suburbs. A pall of pollution is often the price powerless inner-city suburbs pay for the convenience of those who demand freeways rather than public transport to maintain their lifestyle. Inner-city kids breathe the lead deposit of the motorists' refusal to submit to public transport. For this reason, we made the car we owned an eight-seater van to help get half the street to school on wet days.

Even in St Kilda, this school was regarded as the least preferable of the options on offer and had an extraordinary range of challenges. Children from homes of abuse and some who had never heard their parents even attempt to speak English were all mixed in with the ragged range of fellow students. The teaching staff had a near-religious devotion to the cause, working long and difficult hours to give many disadvantaged kids an educational chance.

I began by teaching religious education at the principal's suggestion, which had not occurred in the school for many years. Understandably, there was a negative reaction by some of the staff, who noted that in a pluralist multicultural school this could prove exclusivist. I shared this concern, particularly if the religion taught deprecated other religious and cultural traditions, as so much fundamentalist faith that is cut, dried and pre-packaged does.

One teacher was very hostile and I pitched my argument that to deny children the magnificent stories of the Bible was to curtail their cultural life, not to mention religious development. I argued that the seventeenth century had the Greek classics, Shakespeare, and the Bible. The next century shed the classics, but still had access to the cultural resource of Shakespeare and the Bible. The eighteenth century shed Shakespeare and the secularism of the second half of the twentieth century amputated the Bible from the cultural tree. We have been left with the stripped, depleted trunk of TV series like *Neighbours* as the cultural *lingua franca*. These shows had a vocabulary of about 2000 words with no metaphors, similes or historical allusions. How, I asked, were kids to later appreciate Milton, Blake, or any of the poets whose appeal to scripture informed their work? How were they even to read their own Australian historian, Manning Clark, whose anguished wrestle with national (sometimes cosmic) destiny in his history of Australia was incomprehensible without a grounding in biblical allusions? The primary school teacher withdrew her objections.

As a church community, we committed ourselves to the local primary school in all its glorious fallibility. This was no prescriptive command, as education is a highly personal choice and intersects with most parents' deepest aspirations. Universally, we parents regard our labours as building a foundation for our children, and a top education is the ace in the pack to trump others in first access to the game of life. Few want to meddle with this decision or get it wrong. It is one thing to take personal risks as an adult; it is another to experiment foolishly with your children's future.

But a firm conviction among our fledgling community was that a concerted commitment to our area included the choice to not travel to a nicer and safer school. It was gratifying to have that same visionary Principal come to our Christmas service and movingly thank the church families for solidly putting their roots down. A few from the church served as school council presidents, including Merridie, and the local Uniting Church ministers we knew over these years joined the cause with magnificent contributions.

It is at this level that I have often shaken my head at the ambivalent contribution of church schools. The Catholic system built around the Mediterranean village model of parish church and parish school is by far the biggest player in parochial education. But as a product of a privileged Protestant school, I carried a deep ambivalence and I still do.

I have only heartfelt thanks for a first-class education, one which remains an ivy-league education given the staggering dominance of these schools at snaffling the few places in elite university faculties like law and medicine. But I am still unsure of how a church-school education, now inaccessible to the poor apart from the odd scholarship, tallies with the original Christian vision that many were founded upon.

In the State of Victoria, this is exacerbated by the number of private church schools, now one-third of all schools. For some inexplicable reason, this state is the mecca for them. Consequently, far more parents who in other states populate and strengthen the State education system are pulled out of it here. Those backbone families are sorely missed and their resources empower a private-school culture that many believe has nurtured the Melbourne establishment's culture-bearers since the radical nineteenth-century declaration that State education would be free and secular.

Without trawling through the details of this debate, the challenge to the Church is to retrieve her calling. A commitment to quality education is a commendable Christian commitment. But the notion of user pays—the user naturally being the more affluent who can afford quality teaching—is a strange doctrine on the lips of Jesus' followers.

What a prospect if these church schools practised the biblical teaching of the jubilee year, advocated for ancient Israel. The idea is quite simple, but radically egalitarian. After a seven-year period, all debts were to be forgiven, the land rested, and after fifty years all land sold and traded was to be restored to the original owners. Those families that had lost land, their only income-producing unit in an agricultural society, perhaps through unfair trading or the death of the husband, were to reclaim it and make a fresh start.

Imagine if all the Christian schools in Melbourne took their core values from scripture seriously enough to charge enough for an extended period and then use the savings to pay for six years of schooling for students who had no means. Some do already. The cultural impact on the state could be enormous. We might have even some boys from the poor western suburbs applying for membership of the Melbourne Club.

In many schools, the fragmentation of so many families has transferred the teaching and nurturing roles formerly undertaken by parents onto teachers. Such is the stress on families that public debate recognises that schools have become the centres for teaching morality, personal relationships and inter-personal skills. Many parents who treasure these intimacies will be alarmed at state intrusion. But it is obvious in places like St Kilda that there are some feral kids whose homes are war zones that cannot provide adequate nurture. Teachers, not unfairly, complain that every social agenda, from drug and sex education to suicide prevention, gets downloaded onto them. I ask myself, Is this a fair expectation, and are we as a society failing a generation?

The difficult choice of going against the tide

⌁

I vacillate between anger and understanding in my relationship with the wider Church. The anger rises when I see how the choices Christians make are just as self-seeking and self-promoting as those of others. I feel a deep sadness rising within me as so many use pious language to explain how God has called them to be in a big, safe, prosperous church and live in a safe, prosperous area. The number who gravitate to the comfortable eastern suburbs and Bible belt suggests self-comfort rather than the call of God.

But I do understand when I see the cost of trying to swim against the culture. In an incredibly fragmented world where peer-group pressures push impressionable young people toward destructive drug cultures, there seems to be a much greater risk than for previous generations. When our teenage heroes are Kurt Cobain, Michael Jackson or the likes of Marilyn Manson, then I know the frustration of families feeling powerless against these currents. Little wonder they will drive across Melbourne past many churches to get their children into the biggest and best-run youth group to assure them of Christian peers. The growth of these super-churches has a lot to do with this parental anxiety.

Ronald Conway, a psychologist, notes that a generation ago the family was by far the most dominant influence on our children and was backed up by Church and school—and then peers and media followed as formative influences. Now that is nearly reversed, with Church and school having floated away for most as strong, shaping forces, and media and peers replacing them in influence and challenging the family for first place.

I also see how disabling it can be to be too critical of the Church as, for all her faults, she is still the biggest and most impressive player in human welfare both at home and in aid and development overseas. Few other social groups have organised their voluntary members to contribute ten per cent of their income for maintaining an astonishing range of caring programs.

Nonetheless, the claims of faith are radical. They rebuke the anxious need to squeeze everything good out of this life because this is all we have. That anxiety of death, which feeds the greed of many who must experience everything now because there is nothing more, is injurious to integrity and inimical to faith. The jury is still well and truly out on how our choices will ultimately affect our children. We live with the prayer that it is preferable to have parents who remain true to their convictions and live with passion for their calling rather than parents who play it safe and, therefore, muff their lines in the costly but liberating Jesus script.

Our hope is that living with parents who have a passion for life is enlivening for our children. The numbness of so many kids who have everything and yet have no model of passionate engagement is patent. Many of these children will turn up the music to ear-splitting levels to just feel something. Others in the various punk and youth scenes dress in black and look like they are experiencing the tentacles of death already. We are gratified to see how our own children greet and understand psychiatrically ill friends and street people who have regularly found our door, or pass by in the street. Protecting them from harm while at the same time exposing them to the realities of pain and hope alive in the eyes of visitors is a formative privilege.

Commitment has to be learnt. Though words like loyalty, sacrifice, duty and commitment seem to have dropped out of the lexicon for young people, children need to see examples and believe that living for causes beyond their own is an honourable and invigorating choice. The voice that constantly whispers to forget helping others because you cannot make a difference is louder today than a generation ago. A counter-culture resistance nursed in communities of hope is needed.

It has been a stirring challenge to drop anchor and be committed to a local community. Our state has its motto plastered on every new number plate issued. It reads: 'Victoria on the move'. Cynics agree that yes, it is on the move—to sunny Queensland to escape the harsh weather and the even harsher political leadership. The motto is true for all of Australia, with thirty per cent of the population moving every five years, and seventeen per cent moving every year. Our communities are revolving ferris-wheels stopping periodically for some to get off and be replaced by a new bunch of riders.

St Kilda's community is in constant transience and it is hard to start building friendships when people move on. Many of us nostalgically long for the stability of the past, when you progressed through primary and secondary school with the same circle of friends. Of course, we conveniently forget that small, closed communities can also be tyrannous, where one mistake leaves you branded for life. But part of the fascination with retro music and buying Victorian houses and building picket fences is to retrieve something of that nostalgia for simpler communal times. It can be idealised, as Saint Augustine commented: 'Those who long to be back in the good old days only do so because they never lived in them.' But it is becoming apparent that we are breeding a rootless society whose members have exchanged the rich right of citizenship for the mess of pottage called customership.

Citizenship takes local duties, and in particular neighbourliness, seriously. But if one is always on the move, it becomes increasingly difficult to attend to those duties. Our career choices must leave time for citizenship and, most importantly, allow local stability. The pay rise offered to many to move and uproot is not worth the effort having to rebuild all over again. Of course, often there is no choice but, where there is, I recommend digging in rather than taking the dollars and disappearing.

The need for community in an age of insecurity

A paradox which I have never unravelled is the extraordinary hunger in people for community but an extraordinary unwillingness to pay the price of building it. So many community organisations are in deep crisis. Volunteers are not there in the numbers they once were, as an individualistic blight eats at our communal energy. Looking inward rather than beyond ourselves is explained as compassion fatigue, or paralysis of information.

Australians are giving less to either local or overseas aid. Foreign aid as a national percentage of GDP has fallen to its lowest levels in our history. We are shamed as a nation of mean-fisted tight wallets when compared to Dutch, Scandinavian and other comparable middle-sized powers and budgets. Both major political parties have gloriously covered themselves in shame on this score. Yes, this may pass for political responsiveness to the national mood in our leaders who are only reflecting the narrow parochialism and self-centredness of this affluent nation, but they do deserve stick and opprobrium for their moral cowardice.

Although Australians today are much more affluent than their parents were, they do not feel it. The news that the average levels of savings needed to buy a house or car is far less than in previous generations does not prompt greater generosity. Why? The reasons are probably complex and may embody the old adage that the more you have, the more you want. But, equally, they may reflect the yawning insecurity Australians are also experiencing. Today their jobs, their marriages and therefore their futures all feel insecure. Yes, you can make more, but you can lose it fast, or can be caught between jobs in debilitating unemployment. Alan Bond has taught us that huge monies are no hedge against spectacular ruin and bankruptcy. How fickle and insecure wealth is.

In such an epoch of insecurity, individuals hunger for belonging and community. The rage of tracing family roots and understanding the social and cultural influences that have intersected with your genes is a 'belonging' urge. I observed this in my daughter's fascination at my mother's sixtieth birthday. Three of us were deputised to speak about her. Her brother, a Federal Court judge, told tales about her demotion as a school prefect for giggling on the tram and other shocking deeds of the first period. My father spoke about the second twenty years, rich in humour and pathos. I spoke on the last twenty years. All the time Claire, who was seven, had an absorbed look on her face and pocketed every funny story and incident. For the next three months, she trotted out the stories and relished retelling them. She was finding her place in the family through the experiences of her grandmother. She was claiming her birthright, her point of belonging.

But the aching for security is like Dr Doolittle's 'push you pull me'. It pushes people to lament their few real roots and long-term friendships, but pulls them from serious commitment for fear of entanglement.

Community groups that had their high noon in the seventies are languishing. A professionalised world suspects volunteerism to be unprofessional. Is their public liability sufficient to take my child on camp or to this activity? Why would people give their most guarded possession, time, for voluntary programs? Churches were run by women whose life destinies as networkers, nurturers and housewives were the dominant cultural choice. But that reservoir of pastoral labour has virtually evaporated as they have re-entered the workforce and become secularised (the group leaving the Church in greatest numbers is career women).

The Church is a richly resourced body and a social and spiritual institution with a certain status in society. When I ponder its future in a climate where many are sceptical and saying no to its institutionalism and tradition and are unsure about its wealth, I think of the biblical story of Zaccheus. He was a wealthy tax collector with a certain status, even though his gains were ill gotten. Yet he yearned for spiritual truth and yearned so strongly that he was not averse to climbing a sycamore tree to see the preacher from Galilee pass by, surrounded by a great throng of followers. Jesus stopped and looked up at him and said, 'Come down. I'm coming for dinner.' The heartstopping acceptance and grace was too much. As he scrambled down, Zaccheus publicly announced that he would restore the losses to those he had ripped off by repaying them fourfold. Jesus announced that this day salvation had come to Zaccheus. An alternative for 'salvation' would be integrity. Jesus directly implied that integrity had dawned in Zaccheus' home and this was good news for the rich.

The Church, rich in wealth, must recover her integrity, as her respect and influence were not historically transmitted, but won through life-changing service and a radical sharing of wealth.

Moving on
～

After six years of living in and on Marriott Street, we began to feel our energies were drained and that we needed a bit more space for our growing children and their antics. We carefully watched every house within the block and in early 1992 one came on the market, literally around the corner, which offered a backyard of sorts, an extra bedroom, and, perhaps most importantly, a measure of psychic space, without removing us from the neighbourhood.

We did what everyone advises you to do and bought it before selling our home. It was a stressful couple of months, but a great band of friends pitched in to repaint our place in a week. Going through the open inspections was a nightmare, especially with three young children, but somehow, despite a dismal result at the auction, we found a buyer shortly there-after. And so, in August 1992, we walked our belongings around the corner, and within a few hours nearly burnt the new house down. Someone had placed all the linen up against a faulty and illegal heater vent, and while we all busied ourselves the towels started to smoulder away. It was a grand introduction to Argyle Street—a smoke-filled house, screaming children and three fire trucks, sirens blaring, bringing all our new neighbours out to watch and greet us.

And so the journey continued, a different street but the same network, the same needs, the same joys.

six

Building a healing community

Ivan Illich was once asked what is the most revolutionary way to change society. Is it violent revolution or is it gradual reform? He gave a careful answer. Neither. If you want to change society, then you must tell an alternative story, he concluded. We know a deep world-weariness at the tastelessness of the dominant consumer culture, but locating the alternative life-giving 'story' is proving hard work.

In Australia, our story of the past is of a harsh, unromanticised struggle, often tinged with great sacrifice in a continent whose searing interior heat and dryness, followed unpredictably by torrential rain, defeated the pioneers with bushfire, flood and drought. The vastness of the land produced a deep, brooding, ageless silence which the Aborigines saw as resplendent with meaning, but which we Europeans identified with meaningless suffering and cruel fate. Unlike the more romantic American experience of triumph over a rich continent, fighting a worthy foe in the native Indians, struggling with noble themes like liberty from England and the human slave trade, we were a penal colony whose explorers were beaten back to the coastal fringe, leaving the interior to the Aborigines. Our heroes are magnificent failures like the Anzacs at Gallipoli, the bushranger Ned Kelly, and the explorers Burke and Wills.

We are terrified of the Great Emptiness and what historian Manning Clark described as the Kingdom of Nothingness descending.

Few individuals seem to have a cause large enough to motivate them. Most settle into passive mediocrity, satisfied to be trivialised to death by the lure of the latest consumer gadget. A ludicrously large advertising industry applies astounding research and creativity to cultivating the appetite for these consumer tranquillisers. It aims at making us feel dissatisfied with the way we look and what we've got. Then there is the television news presented by hosts who anchor it as entertainment, a style known as 'infotainment', which has become the preferred form of civic discourse. However, as with the incessant chatter of talkback television and radio that adores this style, we know it is little more than an endless form of baby talk. Pictures with ten-second grabs are seriously offered as news—an alchemy of analysis and information.

Restless activists grope around looking for the action and picking up disparate causes and then dropping them for more novel ones. The death of the grand narrative, whether it be Marxism, Freudianism, fascism, the myth of progress or a bene-volent all-powerful God, is a chilling death. The vacuum created is enormous and lots of half-thoughts and half-causes float in like torn fragments to occupy the empty space. None satisfies. George Johnston in his marvellous novel *My Brother Jack*, set in the suburb next to St Kilda, said that the 1930s was the last period when great causes motivated people. He described two friends, fellow journalists, sharing a ship's berth over to Spain, one to fight with the socialists and be killed, and the other, a militant Catholic, to fight for God and General Franco's fascists.

Some believe that we are in transition between major theories of understanding reality, the sort of transition that comes along only once every three hundred years. They knowingly assure us that the pain of transition will yield to a new way of being; a sort of new intellectual Aquarius. Maybe, or maybe not, but it sure is confusing in the meantime.

Those sensitive to truth and longing to be free blame the emptiness they feel on the suffocating religion of secularity that has provoked a near-total loss of spiritual transcendence. Secularists have convinced us that God has left the phone off the hook. The absence of spirit is acute. The less sensitive seem comfortable in their smugness that nothing can touch their consumer affluence and look uncomprehendingly blank at the suggestion that we might submit to the awe and mystery of a divine spirit. The advent of crystals, astrology charts and a plethora of New Age courses and books in spirituality is a response to the arid tracts of technical reason.

We have experienced a wholesale cultural 'unplugging' from a meaning mainframe, and we compute life without any sense of direction or destiny. I heard a speaker tease out the modern anguish with this snapshot. A lifelong communist, who had fanatically believed in the revolution and the inevitability of history moving towards a classless society, lay dying. On his death bed he lost his lifelong faith, recanted his atheism and abandoned his belief in Marxism. He called for the priest and was baptised, abjuring all atheism and revolutionary fervour. He died, reconciled to God and the Church. His family gathered to read his will and were surprised that he had left everything to the Rockefellers. If there is no grand purpose or meaning left, then choices need not make sense.

An immediate personal effect is the loss of belief in anything. It is a sobering conclusion to admit that there is nothing that seems worth committing your life to. No cause is moral enough to die for. Images of Balkan fighters self-destructing for love of tribe register as monstrous patriotic fanaticism. But both Australian Serbs and Australian Croats who have lived in peace with each other out here enthusiastically signed up to wage murderous war for this patriotic cause. At last, there was something to die for. Similarly, American boys went off to the Gulf in 1991 to die for democracy, although a stubborn suspicion circulated that the loss of cheap petrol for their Chevvies (should Hussein keep Kuwait's oil reserves) was the real moral issue. The loss of democracy has never been a flash enough argument to warrant NATO military intervention in countless other places.

The existential dilemma of feeble, uncompelling causes is great. Life seems to be the triumph of the cautious and fainthearted. What do you commit yourself to when every belief is subjected to ruthless and exacting attention that mocks and demystifies it? Ideals are shattered through cynical analysis. Anyone who has even a whiff of idealism about them is subjected to exhaustive scrutiny to show that they could not possibly be living up to these ideals.

Whilst those who profess one thing and practise another should be exposed, it is hard to swallow the self-righteousness of the iconoclastic bounty hunters who challenge every dreamer. Their clever, buttoned-down cynicism is equally destructive. Is it not so easy to tear down and so problematic to build up? It is a world where there are no mysteries to honour, but only problems to be solved. It is hard to believe and find renewed energy.

A fragmented way to start
⮩

That rather depressing description more or less captures the climate, and to a lesser extent our spiritual state, when we began work in St Kilda. My theological education, though I was immensely grateful for it, had relativised my faith. Its disciplines approached the biblical text with critical tools that seemed to deconstruct rather than reconstruct the intended meaning. This stretched faith to the point of snapping as old, loved biblical interpretations were crudely dispatched. Fresh from a theological battering of our assumed worldviews about the omnipotence and benevolence of God in the face of Dachau and Buchenwald (which we visited), I see now what a tough legacy this was with which to start out in ministry preaching to a small elderly congregation who enjoyed a pre-modern faith. In hindsight, we see how depressed we were with the post-modern disease of not quite believing anything with passionate assurance.

We experienced the fragmented existence of St Kilda as needing binding together, and experienced our own frag-mented lostness as needing wholeness. The very questions of why a church exists or what a religious outlook has to offer are difficult to answer in the face of triumphalist secularism and rampant cynicism. The Latin root of the word 'religion' means *to bind together*. Symbolically, the demonic is the opposite. It means to pull apart and fragment. That was spot-on in our attempts to make connections between faith and family, faith and law, faith and government, faith and local community. Our core was our faith and out of it emanated the desire to link life's parts, fragmented though they seemed to be.

However, we had discovered that much of our received faith was too rigid to incorporate contradictory experiences. Here we were turning over new experiences and insights and these complex data were being fed into our information bank, but the beliefs program in use was showing a system error. The program clearly was in overload and could explain some things, like the need for personal conversion, but not address public conversion. It was strong on exhorting prayer, worship and a moral lifestyle, but removed from economics and local government and a civic ethic.

A cracking open of our categories is simultaneously an experience of liberation and fear. Grief accompanies the loss of treasured understandings and fear is instinctive when you realise that an unseen undertow has caught you and that you are swimming well beyond the flags. But there is also the liberation of knowing that you are free and that in the big, wide ocean you remain alive and carried by unknown currents.

A second pastor in the St Kilda church

～

Limping into ministry without any grand strategy is not a recipe for success. We stumbled into courses of action rather than intelligently trying to plot each move. I was trying to bring together the strands of law and theology through a pastoral practice in both the church and legal office and soon realised that I was not able to cope with both. Though we had seen about forty people join us, we were still a small church when I set out to convince them to call a second pastor to help with the ministry.

Now for a congregation who had just twelve months earlier welcomed their first permanent pastor in a couple of decades, and whose size meant that the absence of a couple of members would reduce the offering by nearly twenty per cent, it took a quantum jump to understand why they now needed a second minister. To the old political question of where would the money come from, I had two answers. First, we would trust God, and second, we would support ourselves as worker-priests.

We called Bill Hallam, an old friend who had spent the previous few years leading a remarkable community in Amsterdam.

This was a community of about fifty people living on two leaky old houseboats, called the Ark, on the canal at the back of the main Amsterdam railway station. Its living quarters, mostly below waterline, were awfully dank and cold, particularly in the long Dutch winters, but the life and fellowship above water level was warm and dry. This community took in the broken and hurt and nursed them back to health—and often to Christian faith. Travellers who got robbed of money and passports, Irish provisionals on the run from the Brits, druggies trying to make a clean start, and international wayfarers with a host of visa irregularities found refuge in the Ark. Like Noah's original life-preserving voyage, this community offered hope and shelter in the deluge of distress.

Bill, with his wife Christine, began community-outreach ministry as a pastor in St Kilda. He took up some part-time house-painting to support his three children, a son followed by twin girls who had been born just months before they came. His strength and wisdom soon saw many broken people circulating in his orbit for help.

One of the traditions that had been enjoyed on the Amsterdam Ark was a special meal called a love feast, a meal that broke with the plain food that a tight budget dictated—they lashed out with some trimmings. In our context, it became an inclusive time that brought together the core of the church with all who cared to join us. A meal that is free includes everyone—and the poor know they are welcome.

Some friends we had made, who suffered with various disabilities, lived in special accommodation hostels and relished the opportunity to come along to the 'parties', as they called them. Sitting at table together were middle-class, tertiary-trained young adults and drug-addicted, sex-addicted, homeless and psychiatrically ill people. In our fragmented world, this was a breathtaking sight. It was a foretaste of Jesus' vision of the kingdom where all are invited and each has a set place at the high table.

Yes, the name love feast did raise an eyebrow or two in St Kilda. However, the rich biblical feeling of an agapic love meal, which celebrated the gift of community that the death and resurrection of Jesus granted, was worth the risk of misunderstanding. Love feasts remained an inclusive monthly meal that was followed with a fun theme night until the occasion grew too big to fit into the church.

The social trends in St Kilda in the 1980s

ᴖ

Inner-city areas are the social laboratory where the trends sweeping the world's cities hit first. These eventually wash out to the suburbs, whilst the pattern begins again with a new wave washing over the inner city.

The social trade winds had dumped a particularly interesting load in St Kilda in the mid-1980s. St Kilda had long been a magnet for runaway kids to play the pinnies and doss down in the squats. For those who got entrenched, there was quick sex as a means to make an income of sorts. The rule of the streets was rip others off before they rip you off. Trust no-one.

The same jungle lore applied to those in the drug trade, as the chemical fix hyped up or hosed down deadened eyes and abused bodies. A different type of homelessness was on the increase and we soon learnt that the humane policy of deinstitutionalisation, namely closing down our cold psychiatric wards, had an inhumane side effect. They were living on the streets. The government funds to provide supportive community housing and care were not there, and unscrupulous profiteers in the worst boarding houses in St Kilda picked up the new housing demand.

Another first was the human immunodeficiency virus (HIV) which was just penetrating our consciousness as the next epidemic. St Kilda has many gays and over fifty per cent of Victoria's HIV-positive people. But ignorance and fear abounded and the Reverend Fred Nile was reminding people that he could see all the signs of a visitation of the wrath of God in this plague. In our experience, this only entrenched the worst images of a vengeful God firing off cosmic darts at those who displeased him. Furthermore, it cut the sufferer off from spiritual resources in their time of greatest crisis. Many conservative groups hit the streets of St Kilda proclaiming God's judgment on gays, and many heated arguments ensued.

Breaking the connection between sex, death and God's judgment is always difficult. It is made more difficult by the fact that this particular transgression was highlighted. I did not hear these same Christians, for example, arguing that a person with lung cancer was being punished or judged by God for their smoking.

I became involved in the National Churches AIDS Group that sought to influence the wider Church away from this proscriptive and heartless thinking. I am glad to say that the mainstream Church never bought this vindictive theology, at least not officially or publicly.

The first man I knew who was dying of AIDS came to the church in 1985. He was dreadfully thin and desperately alone. His father had rejected his homosexuality and thrown him out of home years before. He had lived without family supports

and without any permanent partner. As his condition deterio-
rated, I tried to help him reconcile with his father—which was,
literally, his dying wish. I discovered in his father a man who
could not and would not lower any of his barriers towards his
son, even in the last moments when his son felt utterly alone.
The father's fear and repulsion was stronger than love or
compassion and he could find no forgiveness or acceptance in
his heart. I sought all too inadequately to fill the void and saw
this dying man regarding me, a minister, as representing the
Fatherhood of God, one who loved rather than pushed away.

AIDS has challenged the whole ministry of the Church.
For decades, the Church had been mocked in some 'progressive' quarters for presenting the Bible's ancient teaching
against promiscuity and premarital sex as a killjoy, *passé* ethic
that did not understand how the pill had delivered a liberating
sexual revolution and furnished humans with new possibilities
for personal pleasure. With the advent of AIDS, these timeless
teachings jumped out of the category of restriction into life-
saving and life-giving morals. The twin pillars of fidelity and
chastity have regained a claim as absolutely beneficial for
health and relationships.

But AIDS has also exposed the Church's weakness in
thinking about sexuality and God. The long ambivalence
toward sex, starting with Augustine and continuing through to
Aquinas, followed a path that explained the universality of sin
by linking it to human conception. Since all humans came into
existence through intercourse, that must be the point of con-
tamination with original sin. This completely ignored the
declaration in the Genesis creation story that sex, represented
in the creation of maleness and femaleness, was declared
unequivocally good.

This ambivalence towards sex has complicated attitudes to

HIV, which can be communicated by intercourse. Sin and sex are again unhelpfully linked, rather than sex being seen as a majestic gift of God.

The establishment of a house of refuge
—

Our work was in full swing by 1986 and it was all too apparent that the work of counselling and caring was helpful for some, but too piecemeal to see breakthroughs. Addictions of all kinds were dreadfully resistant to help, and life skills were not going to be taught through one hour of counselling a week, no matter how good we were at it.

We started looking for a large house to build a community that could take in some heavy-duty people who needed more care than a counselling session permitted. One of the couples who joined us in the beginning were Ross and Lyn Dickson, whom we had originally met in our days as youth pastors at Oakleigh Baptist Church. In 1977 they were newly married and on the verge of buying their first home in Bacchus Marsh, on the very outskirts of Melbourne. Somehow we clicked as good friends and they felt inspired to stay on and journey with us. In the intervening years, while we were in Europe, Ross and Lyn had spent some years in Goa (India) running a house for Western drug addicts who needed to detoxify and be repatriated home. They had magnificent personal skills and were willing to attempt a costly communal lifestyle in St Kilda, even though they now had two young daughters. Coincidentally, a legal client of mine had heard of this vision for a house and indicated she would put up half the deposit. We were fussy enough to stipulate that it needed to have a self-contained flat on site to give the Dicksons space from the seven-day-a-week ministry.

After some months of fruitless searching for a suitable place, I saw an ideal property of six bedrooms with a second-storey flat on top. I rang Ross, who was our church secretary at the time, and suggested he and our legal client go to the auction to see what it went for. I said by no means bid and was disappointed that we had not seen it in enough time to have a church meeting to approve bidding for it.

On the day of the auction, I went off to the football like most football-fanatical Melburnians do and came home to a distressed phone call from Ross. He was ringing to inform me that he was resigning as church secretary. Mystified, I asked why and he ashamedly told me that our legal client had cajoled him into purchasing and signing an unconditional contract in the church's name. I told Ross not to breathe a word of this to anyone.

The next day after church, I called an unconstitutional church meeting and slightly gilded the lily by saying the church had a wonderful 'option' to buy this property. Although it was a close call, as we did not have the money in hand, the church approved us going ahead on a contract they were unknowingly bound to. After the vote, I remember seeing beads of perspiration and sheer relief on Ross' face. Lyn told me later he lost weeks of sleep over the episode. It took a few years before we could openly talk and laugh about it.

We chose the name Machaseh House, which is Hebrew for 'refuge', as it was plonked in a very traditional Jewish quarter. The name best summed up the vision we were carrying for it. Two single adults from the church joined the Dicksons and a very special ministry was born. The first inhabitants came from the Oslo Hotel, one of the grottiest boarding hostels in St Kilda at that time. The Oslo began life in 1861 as a magnificent three-storey terrace known as Westbourne Terrace, but had slipped a long way from those glory days.

'Warren' was living in an outside room at the Oslo with an open sewer a metre from his bedroom. It got blocked on wet days and I will spare you the detail of what floated by his door. I remember visiting Warren and discovering that he desperately wanted to get out but, suffering low esteem from a foster home and a low IQ, he had no real idea how. He jumped at the chance of belonging to an extended family at Machaseh House. Along with Warren, others from drug and disadvantaged backgrounds bunked in and soon a community of twelve to fifteen members were sharing their lives.

The philosophy was pretty simple: through the rhythm of community life, broken lives could be healed. We knew that it took much more than words of advice to break addictive lifestyles; for a start, most came with ingrained reverse living habits. They slept during the day and came alive at night. To many in St Kilda, this made good sense as all the exciting illicit stuff happened at night. So why would you ever sleep then?

The house was not high pressure or crammed full of programs. It was deliberately pedestrian in tone to ground people in a particular way of living. Routine and skills, such as cooking and cleaning, are only learnt by modelling them. Many have never acquired the most basic skills, such as domestic budgeting. So the unemployment cheque never went the distance, leading the person to believe that illegal earnings were the only way to survive. To model alternative ways of resolving conflict rather than punching someone's lights out is demanding work, but unless it occurs, homelessness often results. The skills to live with someone, maintain a relationship and sustain lower rent through a house-share are not there.

Renting on one's own is often not an option because of the expense.

The rules of Machaseh House were equally simple. No drugs, no alcohol, and everyone had to eat evening meals together unless there were special circumstances. Each Monday night was a family time where there would be a sharing around scripture and personal experience. Those who were unhappy with anything happening in the house could raise it and deal with it in the open.

This required great skills of negotiation and mediation. Ross and Lyn stuck to the marvellous principle that conflict is an opportunity for growth if handled with integrity. Most preferred to smash someone's face in or, equally unhelpfully, bury their grievance or wait for it to go away. That usually only prompted a further festering. To be committed to people sufficiently to allow them to speak out their hurts is to offer healing and the security that they can face them. The knowledge that the leaders will not evict or reject you for expressing your feelings is to feel in a truly safe place.

It was this safe place that Machaseh House became. To see Warren and so many others cooking meals for the mob, laughing and socialising together, was deeply moving. Though burdened with their own problems, they had profound insights into their comrades' vulnerabilities and looked out for each other. A number shook off years of self-abuse and contempt and found strength for phenomenal growth. Others found deep faith in a loving personal God, and others started well but checked out for a variety of reasons.

The secret of the house was its normalcy. To have Ross and Lyn and their daughters eating meals in the community was a unique intimacy that some had never known and others had not seen for a long time. Again, we understood that hope and respect is kindled not by programs, but through relationships. Relational sharing in its laughter and necessary confrontations alone fills the void. A few years later, when we surveyed past residents, a number wrote that the most important thing about living at Machaseh was seeing the example of Ross as a loving dad.

'Jeanette' was a fifteen-year-old who came into the house to escape her pimp. He was a heavy trafficker, providing her heroin and a roof, and in exchange, taking her street earnings. He was also a heavy-duty thug and regularly bashed her for not performing, or for spending the money before he saw it. I discovered that Jeanette had a stable middle-class family in the eastern suburbs, but had fled at thirteen and lived a lifetime in the last two years. Her reason for fleeing was so seemingly minor as to be incredible. Her mother was a career nurse who from early days told Jeanette that she wanted her to follow in her footsteps. Jeanette was adamant that she did not want this and so she ran away. The conditional love of home was exchanged for what she might find on the street. She attempted to buy unconditional love and ended up selling herself.

There were many times that we thanked God for Machaseh House. Its large size could absorb people who could find their own niche and friendships and who would have become too intense on their own. It had the staying power that a nuclear family could not provide. Whilst our family and others in the church provided accommodation for people going through pain, it had to be on a short-term basis. Our ability to provide the longer attention they needed was inadequate. Machaseh cared for people for up to two years. A larger family grouping granted greater reources and therefore a better balance of care because the responsibility did not fall continuously on the same people.

It was satisfying to see that deeply troubled people could reach out to others and extend themselves. This non-professionalised family built self-esteem as members levitated out of the confining prison of their own self-obsession and helped others in the house who were doing it hard. Therapeutically, this minimised their own problems.

One French woman was found by a woman in our church literally beaten up and drunk on the footpath outside her home. She was living with a violent Australian, trying to obtain the necessary immigration points to get permanent residency. He tired of her drinking, abused her and evicted her onto the street. The time for 'Ulla' at Machaseh House was just right to face the awful truth that she was an alcoholic. Her natural competence in organising, listening and caring saw her virtually start running the house. This rebuilt her shattered dreams and prompted her to seek solid help at Alcoholics Anonymous. She came through a remarkable battle to regain her dignity and sobriety.

There were the close calls when everything could have been lost. Some neighbours were none too pleased to have a house full of druggies on the mend and knockabout types. Suspicions fed by rumours about who inhabited the place were not uncommon, as it just smelt abnormal to some neighbours.

One of Warren's visitors was, unbeknownst to anyone in the house, a pyromaniac. Ross saw from his upstairs flat this guy jumping over the neighbour's fence and a trail of smoke wafting up from the place he was exiting. He tore down, hurtled over the neighbouring fence and put out the gathering fire. This neighbour had been one of the chief complainants; he was utterly ignorant of who had started the fire. He was so grateful for Ross' quick work that he became a firm friend and ally of the house from that day forth. God moves in mysterious ways!

Another time, an ex-boyfriend of 'Cathy', a nineteen-year-old woman who had joined the house, turned up with a gaggle of mates. Cathy had made it clear that the relationship was over with this man, so Ross came out to break the news that they had better keep going. The ex-boyfriend fired up at this rejection and his mates egged him on to take Ross out, saying they would back him up. He threw a few punches only to be peremptorily floored by Ross' best left hook. He looked around for help, but his brave mates had sized up the mean glint in Ross' eye and hoofed it out of there.

The ex-boyfriend was furious at their treachery and cowardice and asked Ross if he could make a phone call. He got off the phone, smugly muttering he'd fixed them, that they were in a stolen car and that he'd just reported it to the police. His jaw dropped when Ross told him that the police would probably charge him also with the theft. He turned up at my legal office a few days later imploring me to represent him.

Establishing a house of hope
⤙

Whilst we enjoyed a rich sprinkling of all types at our services, we usually had the professionals in charge. Worshippers might have to flex with a highly unusual congregation, but the more nervous members, who believed things could easily rock out of control, at least knew that a qualified 'theological pilot' had a firm grip on the joystick. Professionalism, as a way of harnessing expertise, has its place. But when it comes to empowering people to control their own lives, it also has its clear limitations.

We had learned early that it is counter-productive to tell people what to do. First, they resent it, and second, they only end up blaming you if things go wrong. Much of church

ministry, particularly preaching, can easily degenerate into telling people how to live. Rather, they need to observe and learn
informally and then they can own their decisions about painful
personal change. To that end, we talked long about a centre
where the street people might have more control of their
worship life and their own community. We took over a drop-in
style ministry from a denomination that had closed its operation
and reopened it as the House of Hope.

Its name was chosen after an exhaustive ballot by the street
mavericks who staffed it. Hope points to the future. Most of
these people were living out of their angry and hurt past. Some
had once had money and been ripped off and had decided to
never hold onto it. Others had never got out of debt, drugs,
unemployment, or just general trouble to even think of a future.

Other meal programs in St Kilda gave free meals and
handouts, but there is no end to material needs. We wanted to
try and break that welfare-handout mentality and sheet home
personal responsibility, which is critical to pursuing a future. We
decided to charge for our evening meals and to offer in-kind
work if one could not pay. We made it clear that this was not a
place where you came, got your meal or your own way and
nicked off. If you did that, you were ripping off others you knew,
not some remote Church authority that had plenty of wealth.

Seeing street people enforcing meal payments and backlogs
of duties in a colourful, aggressive style (threats of kneecapping
were not unheard) was to see their way of saying, 'Respect this
place—it is ours.' Since it was their place, they bent their backs
to renovate a derelict property that needed strenuous efforts
to repaint, rebuild and furnish.

The welcome sign went up and the doors opened on a
unique ministry in St Kilda. Nathan Nettleton, a theological
student and member of our church with a gambler's coolness

in crisis, was the only paid coordinator. But the unpaid staff for the seven-days-a-week drop-in all came from the street. The coordinators who cooked for up to forty street people each night of the week plus breakfasts, collected the monies and resolved the fights, all came themselves from the street.

Many of the wiser heads gave this naive experiment a short lifespan. Experience was the best teacher and her lessons were carved into granite: that druggies cannot be relied on, people with prior dishonesty offences cannot be trusted to handle money, and those whose vices were legendary cannot be expected to know anything about running a house of God and worship. We were trusting people in the very areas where they had failed before. Without diminishing that universal experience, the House of Hope has radically challenged a number of those assumptions.

Admittedly, it was a special context. First, we were upfront with the group, saying we did not have the money to run this on a professional basis and we did not intend to worry ourselves sick managing it. If they wanted a safe place to eat and relax and worship, then it was over to them to help establish it and own it. A remarkable burst of energy was focussed on renovation, in the form of the skills of people regarded as unemployable. The next step was asking the group to gather and write their own Bill of Rights—the principles that should govern the house.

Surprisingly, long-term substance abusers emphatically insisted that no drugs were to be tolerated, and guys with histories of violence vetoed any heavy stuff. Treating others with respect and not rejecting them were high on the list of fundamental rights. The hurt of rejection was the common experience of just about all. The Bill of Rights was settled, printed and hung on the wall as the binding covenant. The house was to be treated as a special place that called for special behaviour and that allowed them the possibility of acting differently and, perhaps, even becoming different people.

We may well assume that the only future for people like this is to save them from their world and ship them out of St Kilda. For a number of desperate heroin addicts that is true. They will only end up destroying themselves if they stay in the trafficking networks. But many others need to be saved *in* St Kilda, as the world outside is neither understanding nor welcoming. It is an impossibly lonely existence in the suburbs and those who try to make it feel torn out by the roots and left to wither by the roadside. The street camaraderie in the company of other battlers, even just to bott a smoke, is true fellowship.

The House of Hope demonstrated that the rawest boundary experiences of life can be God-filled. The Sunday-afternoon worship services testified to that. Life in its extremities was surrendered back to God and hope recharged in the midst of many tears.

It is humbling to hand over the leadership of worship not to a trained lay leadership, but to people whose sadness has soaked through to the bone because they know they may never be free of crippling addictions or mental illnesses. A guitarist who wrote his own songs led the music in the worship. He was startlingly creative, and when his illness was unsedated he would play the spirituals on his guitar perfectly, but laughing loudly and uncontrollably even in the saddest song. The others sang heartily, oblivious to the cackling, and respecting that Dave needed a shot of his psychotropic medication.

One of the best natural preachers I have ever heard was a regular at the House of Hope. He was doing a sermon on the text about John the Baptist. He said this heavy dude only wore a loincloth and ate honey and cockroaches. I foolishly interrupted him out of my need for biblical accuracy and said, 'Not cockroaches—locusts.' Before he could correct himself, someone up the back chimed in with, 'Actually, I believe cockroaches are very high in protein.' That triggered another worshipper who said he believed cockroaches were very nice to eat if they were jellied. As debate broke out over the culinary merits of this vermin, our preacher looked at me despairingly and said, 'Sorry, mate, I think I've blown it.' He hadn't—I had. Fortunately, the sermon got a second wind when cockroaches on the dinner table exhausted itself.

I filled in as the coordinator for a period of three months. In my first week I was called in for a tribunal hearing. Now I have been in many quasi-judicial tribunals, but nothing had prepared me for this. If a person broke the Bill of Rights, then they were suspended and had to face the tribunal to be readmitted. The tenth right on the bill was that of a fair trial for breaching any of the other rights, like no violence, no drugs and alcohol.

Brent had been caught dealing some dope in the house and was summarily suspended for three weeks. His tribunal hearing was set and Vinnie, Mick, Alan and Chris were his judges. Under the Bill of Rights, he had to be tried by his peers. This was a new twist on the jury system of judgment by your peers, as all of them had had significant drug problems. Brent was asked if he admitted the charge. He took momentary refuge in the fact that no doctor had tested the substance he had sold to scientifically certify that it was indeed dope. But the withering glare from Mick and the unsubtle body language from Vinnie convinced him that this line of defence was not worth pursuing. He confessed his breach and forswore ever offending again.

He was sent out of the room so that the tribunal might deliberate. As the newcomer wet behind the ears, I was politely told that all of them, individually, had struggles with drugs, but that was not the point. The House of Hope was their church and it was sacred. Alan looked me in the eye and said, 'It is wrong to traffic dope in church, isn't it, Tim?' I could hardly disagree with that. I asked if they would ring the police if Brent reoffended and they looked startled. No, they all agreed that the police must not be involved. Old Australian attitudes about the flatfoots die slowly. Their proposed sanction would terrify Brent more. They would destroy the dope right in front of him if it happened again.

They were right. When they handed down the verdict that Brent was back in, but at the peril of any future dope on him being destroyed, he looked shocked at the gravity of the threat. I realised how deeply they understood the culture and needed to be trusted with responsibility.

Expectations are everything and I was being forced to modify mine. I was learning that drug problems were not always what they appeared. The number of people who used them as an analgesic to soften the harshness of life was not that different from the middle class whose higher incomes sugared their escapes into holidays, restaurants and hi-fis. An illicit joint was the poor person's choice; a four-wheel-drive, most of which never hit dirt roads but presented the possibility of escape, was a richer person's choice.

This is not an argument for drug decriminalisation, but for tolerance to the despair that the loss of hope and personal dreams prompts. What are vices for the middle class, like excessive drinking, gambling and smoking, are the recreations of the poor. Not many other vices are accessible to them. The sins of gossip and careerism that infest middle-class strata seem less malevolent than drug problems and street life.

The conversation and humour in the House of Hope was

real survival stuff. Over endless games of cards, news of what was going cheap, what accommodation was available, where casual work might be found and where to scrounge a second-hand tape deck all did the rounds. The residents found an abandoned Hi Ace van in a back street and, after a deal with the council, did it up for use as the transport vehicle for the house.

Many a tall story was spun for sheer entertainment. Table conversation disclosed the old Aussie myth of 'Melbourne or the bush'. Many residents were drifters from the bush and identified virtue and hope with getting back to a plain, rustic life. The bush was honest and simple in comparison with the city, which represented vice and entrapment. Even those who had decamped from the bush through unemployment and were now entranced by the drugs and bright lights felt strongly, perhaps a little romantically, that one day when they got life together they would take up their swag and go back there. Australia, according to Donald Horne, was the world's first suburban nation, but the bush ethic of true mateship and redemptive and honest prospects still persists.

Many of the stories of hardship laconically told in the House of Hope were against the city person and for the mateship of the bush. It was as if energy must be preserved for survival in the face of continuing adversity. William Hughes, a regular of the house, was the embodiment of these values. He had lost three fingers on one hand and was never seen without his bush cap and cockerel, whose wings he had clipped. It fluttered and querulously relieved itself on his shoulder. He had painted some magnificent pictures of the outback, some in Aboriginal style, for an exhibition. For a time these decorated the drop-in centre's walls. He dispensed warmth and exuded bush values in the heart of the inner city. As in the bush, a couple of dogs were always in the house and were playfully teased and fed (despite health rules about animals in places of food preparation). They were a critical therapy and were first step to rebuilding trust for many who could not relate to humans.

The Australian classic, *Such is Life* by Joseph Furphy, captures the religion of so many in the House of Hope. They could not believe in the Jesus of stained-glass chapels and choirs, but confessed '. . . the grave truth . . . the Light of the world, the God in man, the only God we can ever know, is by his own authority represented for all time by the poorest of the poor.' This sort of God is a bloke who is on the side of the angels, which they know they are not.

Most residents had experienced religion as rejection. They had felt rejected by their failure to live up to their own standards, let alone trying to vault the high bar of divine standards. Some deliberately tested our acceptance to the limit. Their inner script said, 'I will prove that you people will push me away like everyone else has'—and they did a mighty thorough job of making this a self-fulfilling prophecy. It was sad to see that, for such people, the painful but familiar route of rejection was less scary than the untrammelled turf of acceptance. Such hard-core cases had us expelling them.

But at other times we broke through the vicious cycle and saw tears of grace bathing wounded hearts. Tears are a wonderful solvent for dissolving barriers.

Establishing a place of acceptance

⟶

Part of acceptance is being unshockable. I had grown up believing there were only two standard human models: the male and the female. My first night in the Piano Bar at

St Kilda's infamous Prince of Wales pub taught me otherwise. There were stunningly tall women dressed in micro-mini skirts sleekily sweeping past to some sniggers and a hoarse whisper from someone elbowing me saying, 'Isn't that bloke the best-looking sheila you have ever seen?'

Soon, a woman who was born a man was worshipping regularly at church. He had been homosexual in Europe and copped downright persecution. Upon migrating to Australia, he had resolved the problem by a full sex change, so now his appetite for men was natural! To see her sitting happily next to some of our saints dressed in their Sunday best was to see a picture of a new identity in the family of God.

Soon another transsexual was asking for baptism. In our tradition, this is for adults and by full immersion. He had been a family man with children. Throughout his life, he had felt he was a woman trapped in a man's body and loved dressing as a girl from childhood. He had fervently hoped that marriage would resolve these unsought feelings. Tragically, it didn't and he broke the news to his wife and children that he had finally decided to live as a woman. He lost all contact with them. He came to us as a woman who had discovered faith in Christ. I baptised her after she had checked out carefully whether our church would reject her.

Not all people who undergo sex changes resolve the conflict. I have spent many hours with a man who, pre-operation, had dressed for years as an elegant woman and lived consistently as a female. But since the expensive operation which she had so badly wanted, saved for and meticulously embraced right through the exhausting range of required tests and counselling, she has dressed only as a man. The operation only succeeded in leaving her with more hang-ups than a rotary clothesline. Her agony is intensely public, as she swings like a wild barometer in her feelings and disorientation. Watching her wearing a suit and tie on sweltering hot days is to watch someone punishing themselves for an irreversible decision.

Identity is so fickle. At birth, we are dealt the cards that largely determine body weight, shape and looks. If we have any doubts that this is not a culture commandeered by the beauty myth, we need only note that one of the few industries not to know a sales downturn in the last recession was cosmetics. It thrives as we spend our lives wrestling to conform our bodily imperfections to those internalised beauty images propagated by the culture.

Teenage girls are particularly vulnerable to looks, style and image. Hours each day are spent on discussing and cultivating a 'look'. Of course, the magazines cruelly display computer-retouched models whose cheekbones and features are changed to match the ideal of perfection. These non-human concoctions of ultimate beauty leave fragile, developing egos helplessly envious. Whether the identity issue is as a dramatic as a gender disorientation or as trifling as baldness, it crushes so many.

One of the increasing identity issues is the experience of singleness. The church tends to idealise a family culture, even though its Lord was a single man. Trends to singleness are entrenched as now over fifty per cent of Australians live in households of two or less people. In St Kilda it is even more marked, with forty-six per cent of our residents living alone.

Our church reflected this emerging social mix and at one stage we had over a hundred single adults in our congregation, easily more than those with partners. I remember one of our women leaders tackling the topic of why the wider Church always designated itself as a family when singles felt a little marginalised by this concept. She preached at one service on the topic, 'If God is so good, how come I am still single?'

Tackling the societal and Church view of couples being the norm was to strike a blow for those who, for many different reasons, found singleness their lot. Curiously, the woman who preached magnificently that night was married within eighteen months to a man in the congregation who had heard her.

We prefer the use of the word 'community' rather than 'family' as it is more inclusive and, therefore, more freeing. This is not to deny the reality of singleness or the importance of families, but to affirm that identity is found in relationship, whether we have partners or not.

A community which embodies mutual rights and duties, privileges and obligations is the context for finding true security. The rugged individualist is a nimble economic unit, but allows no self-analysis or insight. Only in engagement with others whom you allow to speak into your life can growth take place.

This sort of community is a gift of grace. It permits enough security to be real because you are known, warts and all. That is the bottom line—reflecting God's acceptance that there is one who knows us completely and still loves unconditionally. Identity founded on that solid bluestone is unshakeable and untouchable by the manipulative guilt industry that says you will never measure up.

Today is quite similar in its existential anguish to the reformer Martin Luther's epoch. Then, the great existential question was posed quite differently, but had the same basic concern with anxiety. It took the form of 'What must I do to be justified in the hands of an angry God?' Justification before God was believed to exist in doing sufficient good works, but one was never sure if enough acts of charity had been performed.

Justification is just as urgent today, but is sought in pleasing or impressing an angry boss rather than an angry God. Performance, whether that be in terms of a contract at work, pressure to perform sexually, to perform in sport—or even in producing happy families—is the way we justify ourselves. Aboriginal society, which we Europeans often regard with contempt for its indolence, has shown us a markedly different way. The word 'work' is not even in the vocabulary of many Koorie languages. People are not accepted by doing, but by being. They are not hung up about achieving and justifying their importance by performance. As part of the clan, they are justified.

Whilst there are strengths in our culture, we have removed any need to justify ourselves in the eyes of a God. We have replaced that tyranny with the awesome need to quarry meaning out of nowhere and prove that we are justified, that we are a success to ourselves. It is a society anticipated eerily by the German philosopher Friedrich Nietzsche in his parable of the madman who appeared with a lantern in the marketplace, looking for God. Because the others did not believe in God, they scoffed at him and asked scornfully where he could have gone. The madman turned on them and shouted, 'We have slain him, you and I; we are his murderers. Do we not wander through an endless nothingness? Does empty space not breathe on us? Is night coming, and even more night? Must we not light lanterns at noon? God is dead. God stays dead and we have slain him.' His hearers could only look on in bewilderment and he finished by saying, 'I came too early; it is not my time. The monstrous event is still on its way . . . This deed is still further from men than the remotest stars—and yet they have done it.'

To assuage the fear of meaninglessness, 'endless nothing-ness', our culture turns inward and asks the great question of life, 'How can I realise my untapped potential?'

Salvation has been redefined to be a fulsome exploration of who I am. The worst epithet that can be applied to one whose life has ended is 'What a waste of their talents!'

Salvation in this culture is no longer about overcoming an alienation from self, neighbour or God. It is not about reknitting the fracture that, from the beginning, has run through human character and through social existence by faith in the reconciling life of Christ. Salvation is reinterpreted as being sufficiently focussed to release all the gifts within and realise that potential. Pity the brilliant person who dedicates her life to the 'irrelevance' of prayer, or working with the poor, because they will never be the movers or shakers.

Egalitarian mateship in Australia prided itself on loyalty to a mate who needed help in a tight spot. Whilst mateship did not quite extend to women or blacks, it finds a resonance in the Aussie breast today. But where mateship decrees that you stick by someone and never run away, I can imagine today's response: 'I have to think of myself and all that I can achieve. I have personal goals. See you later!'

Self-fulfilment may be a personal responsibility, but it is not salvation. Salvation as personal focus on being fulfilled leaves under-achievers unsaved. This tyranny is the opposite of the gracious pronouncement that God in Christ stuck by all of us, his mates, even unto death; that we are justified not by what we achieve, but in being made in God's image and saved by Christ. For me, on this rock, human rights and human charity are founded. That frees us to be self-fulfilled, but not at the price of neglecting others.

Working with children and youth in the St Kilda community

↝

Our worker-priest model saw others join the team. One of the creative opportunities was the calling of a pastor, Jon Charlton, who came to work with youth. Jon is a trained teacher so he started doing voluntary lunchtime work at a local high school. Before too long he was offered the position of student welfare co-ordinator. Pastors being paid by the education department was a first.

Jon's work was with the emerging face of youth homelessness. These were not feral kids who had dropped out completely and graduated to hard drugs and crime, but students who badly wanted to stay at school but had to leave home. The incidence of family breakdown and violence was epidemic and kids were the main casualties. Entrenched patterns of grabbing a bed at a friend's home for a month and then moving on when it got too much for that family were widespread. The full spinout of family lifestyle changes and breakdowns was seen in students lining up for breakfast programs in schools that must feed as well as teach. Machaseh House has turned its attention to providing a home for these students. Seeing teenagers whose family security had come adrift at crucial times in their education find a home and successfully complete their education was exhilarating.

Of course, the reverse side of the homeless coin is the parents who have seen their rebellious teenagers opt out for trifling reasons and spin a line of horrific abuse to trusting social workers who obligingly arrange dole cheques and independent housing. It happens. I have overheard my own children with their friends ring the kids' help line and, with barely controlled mirth, give a plausible plea for help to escape their alcoholic parents and receive a most sympathetic ear. Situations like this have led us to insist on trying to speak to the parents and, wherever possible, work for a reconciliation and return to home. Integrating different sides of the story, even at the risk of breaching total confidentiality, is worth the risk.

Parents need to form their own version of neighbourhood watch. Instead of cooperating vigilantly to protect our videos and computers, we should cooperate to protect our teenagers from a culture that is ravenous in devouring their family life and offering them as adolescents the fool's gold of total independence. The conformism to the peer group's uniformity in dress, music taste and definition of 'coolness' is nearly totalitarian. To protect our kids, we must discuss with other parents what we will accept as curfew hours, party behaviour, alcohol rules, and even expenditure levels on brand labels and accessories. So that when those paralysing words, 'You are totally unreasonable; not at all like my friends' parents' are fired off, we can meet the guilt head on: 'No way. We have spoken with those parents and we all agree that you are must be home by this hour.' Solidarity is always preferable to being picked off one by one by a consumer-sniper culture.

A last refuge for those who doubt

⤳

To recognise the systems of evil that co-opt our self-interest and plunge us into collusive participation is to wonder if living with integrity is impossible. Jesus' admonition that 'narrow is the way that leads to life and few are those who travel the path' is spot on. Little surprise that Tolstoy, who sold his property and gave it to the poor serfs only to see his generosity provoke drunkenness and envy, asked in despair, 'Can anyone live righteously?' Every act has the seeds of destruction in it. However, the road less travelled is the only authentic path, otherwise the cancer of cynicism and self-interest rots our bones.

If Christian faith is to be truly Christian it must eschew the cultural gods of convenience and self-fulfilment to engage with the powers of death that confronted Jesus. By naming and disclosing the illusory nature of those powers that promise respectability, comfort and legitimacy in the name of the dominant culture, there is authenticity and a free space in which to live. That free space permitted Jesus to pray, 'Father, forgive them' for his murderers. When God drinks the cup of hemlock and dies, we see a revelation of the moral and spiritual courage of Jesus of Nazareth. He was crucified in the name of the false imperial Roman powers and the false religious god of rewards and punishment. His life opens us up to the suffering and tragedy of life as well as its triumphs. But this brings doubt. Preachers warn the faithful not to stray too close to the camp of that seductive enemy—doubt.

We saw a number try our church as the last gasp before they give up on God or Church or both. Too often they come wracked by doubt, finding every sermon they have heard can be summarised in two words: 'Try harder.' That has not helped with their doubts concerning the governance of a good God in a world with such pain. They understood faith as an ethics lesson, and another lecture in ethical values at church is not going to soothe their troubled souls.

We had our share of faith crises in our ministry. The mullock heap of belief has come tumbling down on some, crushing former faith and hopes. We have seen that regaining faith in a post-modern world is like standing on the edge of a cold swimming pool. Until you take the plunge you never know whether it will enliven the senses and refresh the whole body or not. This is always the most personal experience and though many have been put off because they have met Christians who are a pain in the *derrière*, we have encouraged all to put that aside to take the plunge and discover the integrity of Jesus Christ.

One of the initiatives we undertook for several years was to organise weekend exposures to St Kilda's subcultures. We called them Finding God in St Kilda and invited groups of six to eight to leave their comfort zones and spend a weekend visiting a range of ministries and people within the reach of our neighbourhood. So a lunch at the Sacred Heart Mission's large meal program was mandatory as were visits to Special Accommodation Houses, and perhaps most pertinently, a night's stay at one of the cheap rooming hotels. The mildew and smells, the sights and sounds always had the profound effect of making people much more aware of the challenge of poverty.

We would spend some time in reflection with these groups afterwards and it was often very moving to see the personal growth that people had undergone as they sought to encounter their own fears, prejudices and self-protectiveness. It was always a sacred journey—for God is there in the midst of the mess and brokenness. It just takes time and courage to be there oneself.

Can the law be

a vehicle of grace?

The second institution to which I have dedicated some years of my life is the law. I began as an articled clerk in 1979 with a small practice in eastern suburban Melbourne. My boss, Alan Moore, had studied law whilst working as a policeman, and then went on to build an impressive practice.

I was his first articled clerk and he was as unprepared for this as I was. He had one rule of thumb that was both terrifying and liberating: there is virtually no mistake in law that cannot be remedied, so I was not to bother interrupting him to seek instruction, but just have a go. That sort of challenge appealed to me.

Pretty soon, I discovered the golden rule for beginning life in a legal office: do not ever, *ever* dare get the secretaries offside. Five years of legal education and erudite reading of obscure High Court cases were useless next to years of on-the-ground practice inside a legal office, covering up for the boss's mistakes. A good secretary saved your bacon countless times. As an articled clerk blundering through my allotted cases, I soon learnt to eat humble pie whilst being rescued from another near disaster by a knowing and somewhat bemused secretary.

I certainly remember my first client as an articled clerk.
Because the boss was in court, I decided to impress this client
by ushering him into the boss's big office that boasted fine
legal prints on the wall and a huge leather chair in front of
bookshelves laden with impressive leatherbound volumes. I
thought this should do the trick to cover my nervousness and
inexperience. It was a car accident—a 'crash'n'bash' as it is
known in the trade. The client was an intense man with a face
like a battered Akubra. As he told his version of the accident,
I took notes and noticed him squeezing every ounce of florid
detail into the account. I felt fairly sure that he was much too
preoccupied to notice my youthfulness. So I relaxed a bit, sat
up and started to confidently lean back in the big leather chair.

Now, having never sat in this chair before, I did not know
that it had a broken hinge. As I pushed back, it took on a life
of its own and kept reclining quickly until I was parallel to the
ground, with my legs waving in the air, wildly trying to rebal-
ance. I swung back down as quickly as I could, intently looked
my client in the face and said, 'Mmmm, that was an important
last point you made.' He seemed completely unfazed and just
kept recalling his passionate version of the event that had
brought him to me.

Life as an articled clerk was a great leveller. They are just
one caste above untouchables. They might make it in becoming
legal Brahmins, but articles are part of a lowly-paid indenture
system designed to inculcate humility. Because I was not permitted to appear in court until admitted to practise as a solicitor,
I was chafing at the bit. I had soon discovered that maintaining
orderly files was not my forte and an office felt like a prison. I
desperately wanted to flex my untried advocacy skills in court.

The perfect cover for a chance to do just that came when
I was filling in for the boss at a stint of legal aid at the local

magistrates' court. A man was to appear on a shoplifting charge and wanted to fight it. With heart thumping, I entered my appearance under the boss's name, hoping the clerk of courts would not recognise me.

The case was called and the store detective proved an admirable witness, quite untroubled by the pecks and pokes of my timid cross-examination. I had watched too much Perry Mason to be daunted by the prospect of defeat. I imagined I would snatch victory from the jaws of hopeless evidence and then explain all to my story-loving boss. I enthusiastically called my client because I had implicitly believed his story. It was to take many appearances before I was to learn the legal outworking of the old doctrine of original sin: just about all clients lie to you and those that don't gild the lily.

My shoplifter was a terrible witness and his lying face was as red as a lobster. The gruff old magistrate found him guilty, fined him and then turned a cold eye on me. I saw my legal career swirling down the sink if he should ask whether I was admitted as a solicitor. Did I detect a contemptuous half-smile curling on his lips at this articled clerk out of his depth? After what seemed an eternity, and to my great relief, he perfunctorily waved me away from the bar table with 'You may leave, Mr Moore.' Fortunately, I remembered my name.

Setting up a legal practice in St Kilda

⤙

After returning from theological study to the same law firm, Alan Moore agreed to the experiment of his former employee, now a clergyman, opening a branch office in St Kilda, operating from the front rooms of the church. Mountains of accumulated dust and mouldy relics of past Sunday school materials had to be cleared out before passable office space appeared. We hung the shingle on one of the church doors and opened in March 1985. There weren't many precedents for us to pore over. It was, we believed, the first and only legal practice wedded to a continuing worshipping church in Australia, with the minister working in both. Sadly, Alan Moore was to die of a heart attack on a squash court within a few months, but his young partner Murray Baird, an old friend of mine from law school, undertook to honour the enterprise. The relationship between our humble branch office and Moores, now a substantial suburban law firm, remains intact.

Our philosophy was clear. We were to cover the overheads, including salaries of a solicitor and secretary, but otherwise do work for free or for whatever people could pay. Our intention was to make legal advice accessible to many who felt locked out by fears of expense or alienation from a mysterious profession. Consequently, rather than a plush office with leatherbound books and chair, we worked in storefront-cramped conditions. The local Community Advice Bureau started sending many people who enquired about legal advice and a steady stream of clients began to make their way to the unlikely office in a church, set amongst warehouses. Naturally, much of the work was legal aid and our fees were often highly dependent on State-funded cases. From March 1985, I worked in the office virtually full-time with a secretary, fitting in church work in all sorts of ways around the edges.

I had observed how intimidated poorer clients were with the language of the law. Concepts that were not necessarily difficult were encased in technical phrases that loudly declared 'no entry' to the public. Naturally, this intensified their sense of helplessness and dependence upon the lawyer, who alone could negotiate this foreign language and intimidating world.

The language in our office was intentionally in the vernacular to permit understanding and demystification. All professions have a mercenary interest in retaining an impenetrable language, but that ultimately serves the profession rather than the client. That is not to suggest that, should all law be expressed plainly and simply, then lawyers would be redundant. Much complexity remains and an important role is assured for those who choose the profession. But the abundance of acerbic jokes made at lawyers' expense is perhaps a thermometer of public scepticism towards their performance or sense of self-importance, not to mention their fees.

Law is a fascinating world which has much continuity with the medieval guilds out of which it grew. Even today, its clubby atmosphere points back to those days where entry was barred to the uninitiated. As a distinguished profession serving society, not just itself, it had strict rules about commercialism.

When I started out, there were what might appear today as quaint regulations about touting for work, which were strictly enforced. The very size of the signs on solicitors' windows was prescribed to avoid any grubby taint of advertising. Barristers still cannot advertise their services or step foot into a solicitor's office. That would compromise their integrity as it might be inferred they were touting for work.

It was unquestioned that this was a monopoly field, and the shock of untrained lawyers intruding into our unchallenged grazing on the lucrative clover of conveyancing was greeted with outrage. Once, conveyancing involved a complex search of the chain of old law titles to validate a title. But with the Torrens land system of consolidating all titles and assuring in a uniform manner that there was valid title, the skill in conveyancing was largely made obsolete. Though most firms had law clerks doing this pedestrian and rather routine work, lawyers were still charging exorbitantly, at solicitors' rates that suggested much greater professional attention than was warranted.

I am sad to say that the noble idea of lawyers training for a profession that serves the highest instincts of a civilised society is not one that beats fervently in all legal breasts today. Lawyers have become business men and women. Lucrative earnings and lateral business opportunities speed many into our law faculties. And the odd episode of *LA Law* has probably helped, too. There would be fewer whose sense of vocation spurred them into dedicating their life to the 'rule of law'.

Most would cringe at the lofty suggestion that they are called to serve justice, yet that calling should be equivalent in importance to a religious vocation. The rule of law in society is like the pinch of salt in a cooked meal. It preserves and flavours. But lawyers have long since let their salt go stale by selling their skills to the highest bidder. Behind the stupendous business deals that are now the subject of criminal fraud charges and convictions faced by Australian tycoons were banks of lawyers advising and manipulating for magnificent fees. Paradoxically, like hyenas feeding off the carcasses, they are there again now prosecuting and defending these tycoons for similar fees. Sadly, lawyers have allowed commercial interests to dominate, and therefore deserve some of the present avalanche of public cynicism.

Lawyers have traded their vision of justice for grubby pecuniary gains. Legal magazines are full of management techniques and most firms 'time-cost', which requires a solicitor to keep a running sheet to bill clients for every fifteen minutes of every day. Management mentality has dictated the amalgamation of many small single-practitioner firms in local communities. Photocopying at exorbitant rates symbolises the shift. The lavish office suites of firms of legal specialists, once more typical of business leaders, is another sign. The rule of law that is vital to the whole community seems a secondary pursuit.

Only now is the right of the profession to self-regulate and refuse any outside scrutiny being challenged. When all other industries have undergone micro-reform, law has remained one of the most unreconstructed areas, testimony perhaps to the large numbers of lawyers who sit on the treasury benches legislating in our State and Federal parliaments. Monopolies and self-regulation are now under threat, but this has been a long time coming.

The abundance of lawyers in parliament sometimes prompts confusion in the minds of those outside. The temper of the thrust and parry of the adversarial system leads many mistakenly to believe that politicians must hate each other. Not so. Part of the reason is that so many parliamentarians are schooled in the adversarial system through a legal training. Emotions are put to one side in the interests of two sides pressing their case as vigorously and objectively as possible, in the belief that this gives the best chance of truth emerging. Likewise, clients are often surprised to see lawyers laughing together after a case over which they have just bitterly fought. I have known clients who have been suspicious of my support for them because I might seem to get on well with the other barrister.

Working in law provides a marvellous exposure to life. Larger-than-life characters step out of fiction right into one's office. Real-life stories are indeed often more incredible than the best story novelists can imagine. Law is a place of confession and a plea for mercy that reveals the extremities of life. Judgment rather than mercy is feared and this provokes soul-searching that is otherwise unplanned.

Consequently, I have often been surprised to find that clients greet me as a physician of the soul as much in my capacity as a lawyer as they would a minister of religion. The world where the sacred canopy of the Church stretched protectively over society, with clergy playing a central role, has dramatically shrunk. It is true that social workers, maternal health nurses, family doctors and even lawyers have more often than not replaced the clergy as the soul-carers. Pouring out stories full of trouble and woe is commonplace.

The specialisation that has gone hand-in-hand with professionalism means that many are rebuffed because the specialist is not equipped to offer more than some passing commonsense platitudes. But the emotionally hurt have often summoned their psychic energy to make an appointment with a lawyer and need to tell their whole story. A lawyer who is time-costing will curtly close down the aspects of the story that are non-legal and suggest a counsellor for those emotional problems, an accountant for the financial and a youth worker for the troubles with the kids. The lawyer's role is to deal with the legal stand in the story.

Responsible behaviour by the lawyer to avoid higher time costs for non-legal matters is nonetheless debilitating for many poor. They feel recycled from this desk to that of another professional, and the energy to trot off to see another specialist is generally absent. They have one pressing problem and commonly feel a compulsion to tell all of it in a narrative form, as in their mind it is not compartmentalised.

Operating a legal practice that serves people's needs

ᴗ

So we decided to turn off the costs meter and allow clients to tell the story that brought them through the door. The wholeness was integral to caring. It allowed the listening ear, a response so frequently absent in the hissing static of modern existence, to be offered. It took a long time for trust to develop in cases such as domestic violence. Clients would often engage in small talk until there was an intuitive feeling that you could be trusted to accept them through the shameful chapters that would unfold. Law became not just a means of solving problems, but of journeying into some of the dreadful secrets of life.

In time, we discovered the loneliness of many lives. Clients would drop in on the pretext of a legal question, but really wanted to chat with someone who was friendly. Our secretaries became multi-skilled as they would have to handle all comers at reception. Some came simply wanting a hug and a cup of coffee. How do you time-cost that? A steady stream were after food or money handouts and others were violent men whom we were representing. One had graphic tattoos of a barbed-wire fence around his neck and he went on regular bashing and arson sprees, but always presented as meek as a lamb in our presence. To avoid trouble, we had to keep reviewing security protocols.

Within a few years of legal practice, we opened a counselling office operating from the same premises. Bill Hallam had added to his theological qualifications a major in psychology and many clients found their way upstairs to begin some serious work on the inner dynamics that had pushed them across the line of the law. Bill started to become a regular feature in the witness box, always soberly distinguishing between those who were motivated mainly by a survival instinct in the face of a criminal penalty and those who saw the bigger picture of personal change and growth. This became an enlarged counselling ministry, with Bill moving into it full-time after 1994.

I believe firmly in this service as it is a wonderful support in times of trouble. However, I suspect that the mushrooming of counselling services is a sign of family and community breakdown. At one level, the rapid growth of counsellors reflects the loss of friendship. Buying a listening ear through a counsellor has become a desperate need. Mick Dundee summed it up best in the box office smash, *Crocodile Dundee*. In New York, he was puzzled that everyone had their own shrink. He laconically asked, 'What's wrong? Don't you people have mates?'

'Sally', one of the legal clients who occupied much of my time and Bill's, was a mother of two who had a chronic alcohol problem. When sober, she was a magnificent and caring mother. Her contact with the church had first come with our Transformers' club for kids. She would help out, although it was a week-to-week proposition whether it would be a sober or drunk leader that arrived.

Sally's father had been a mayor who had died in office. I sometimes felt I was wearing her unresolved anger at a father who died before she really knew him. She had a trait that made her a perennial legal client: her drunkenness was never private. Intoxication in public brought her constantly to the attention of police on charges of being drunk and disorderly. But whenever the blue uniforms arrived, she stacked on a violent turn. The minor charge of drunkenness invariably was coupled with resisting arrest and assault of police.

On one drunken, blurred occasion, it included hurling a knife at the cops. My defence of Sally that day warranted an article in the *Truth*, Melbourne's notorious newspaper rag of 'Headless Body found in Topless Bar' fame. Funnily, I soon discovered which members of the congregation read this scandalous rag, as they commented on the report.

Sally's violence when drunk was directed at anyone she perceived as an authority figure who might be keeping her separated from her kids. When her daughter was living at Machaseh House, Sally attacked one of our solicitors at the legal office with a knife.

The Christmas/New Year's Eve period was always the worst time for her after she lost care and control of her kids to the State. One New Year, after our traditional bush dance, I had a phone call from Sally to say that her house was on fire. I raced around to see flames gleefully licking up the turpentine she had poured down one of the sides. Whilst I was hosing that down, she was around the back throwing more turps over the back section. Some sort of drama would happen in some shape or form each New Year as she tried to eradicate the pain of the past.

After countless court cases and even more alcohol-treatment programs, she was still on the bottle. Her suicide attempts, some in our back hall, were her desperate cries for release from a power she could not control. Court only intensified her alcohol problems and despair.

Many times I wondered whether the legal wig and the clerical hat could be balanced on the one head. Each had its own language and disciplines. I had to be very careful about maintaining confidentialities peculiar to each domain. They were sometimes potentially interrelated, as some clients would welcome the prospect of a supportive church community and join the band of 'jesters' making a corporate religious life together. But for me that meant sometimes mounting the pulpit and gazing out on the congregation and thinking that I knew too much about some of these people. Divorcees, drink drivers and thieves stared back up, eyes wide open with expectancy to hear 'their' lawyer attempt to speak the word of the Lord.

I was all too aware of the risks of confusion of categories. I only had to look at Australian history to see the damage done when clergy doubled as magistrates and ordered floggings, and governors doubled as clergy, read the scriptures and then ordered floggings. It had not been a good start for a church preaching of a loving God.

On a personal level, I felt very good about staying in law. I was joined by a very competent woman solicitor and I distanced myself from day-to-day case management. After a year, as the Church grew and needed more of my attention, I took on court-appearance work exclusively, which worked out to be around a day a week. I must admit that, though the move from law to grace was at snail's pace, I think my law work refreshed me for ministry. There is something intangibly therapeutic about ripping off the clergy mask and plunging into some vigorous cross-examination of the police. The very honorific title of 'Reverend' (from the Old English meaning *reverent*) transfers a heavy burden onto the clergy. He or she must come up with wisdom, spiritual answers, and be seen to exemplify a happy marriage, with charming and delightful kids. As the representative of God dispensing guidance and, in some traditions, forgiveness, any clergy failure *ipso facto* reflects on the divine character.

Then there's the negativity towards God and Church that is projected onto the clergy by those who feel judged or let down. These are heavy-duty expectations; it is little wonder that many clergy crack under the strain and swim to the more self-protective shores of secular employment. Caring for burnt-out clergy is a growth industry. I found an alternative solution. For me, it was keeping a strong foothold in secular employment. Others on our team did the same and I believe it has kept us grounded. Since the Church had been secularised, we did the reverse and brought religion to secular institutions like the law. After all, recognising the dimension of spiritual transcendence in the law is as old as Moses' descent from Sinai.

How a legal practice in St Kilda works
~

A legal office in St Kilda is very different to one in the city centre. Because St Kilda functions like a country town, our service was soon widely known on the networks. But, unlike a country town, St Kilda was fast becoming less a community culture where the teachers, police and shopkeepers all knew each other and worked informally to solve problems.

Once, the local bank managers were family friends, but they had fallen spectacularly from that pinnacle into disrepute, thanks largely to financial deregulation. Greedy lending practices bereft of human kindness, and soaring profits through harsh costing policies, such as imposing bank charges on the poor who had accounts of less than $500, cost them the community's trust. We saw similar trends in law, with firms amalgamating wholesale and preferring lucrative commercial work in huge specialised outfits to solving general problems in small general practices. We were determined to be the loyal 'corner store' that could be trusted.

The subcultures in St Kilda are remarkably self-contained and approach legal problems like they might other problems. Whilst scientific rationalism may be the prevailing intellectual fashion, that has not persuaded some of the subcultures to abolish their astrology charts. I was staggered to meet clients whose world was still dominated by the stars and fears of fate. They were equally staggered to meet a lawyer who did not know his star sign. If he was that ignorant of something so basic, what prospect was there of him being a good lawyer in court? Some would want their cases adjourned to a particular date to make sure the planetary alignment bode well. Others would ask that I ran as a defence the inauspicious astrological features of the times to explain their offence. I found myself trying to remind them what Cassius had said long centuries back: 'The fault, dear Brutus, is not in our stars, but in ourselves.'

Others had life experiences that disposed them to believe that the law was only out to persecute them for no good reason. 'Stretch' was a 200-centimetre, tattoo-covered Maori from Auckland, who had got into a vicious fight at the Prince of Wales pub one Friday night. He had laid a few Aussies low with sharp, clean blows and turned back to finish his beer. But then, to his shock, the coppers arrived and he was charged with assault. He was a bit nervous about going inside as there were a couple of transgressions blotting his copybook.

I managed to keep him out of gaol, and over a coffee opposite the Melbourne Magistrate's Court, he complained bitterly about the police and the inhospitable way of life in Australia. He thought he might go home where things were simpler. I asked him to explain.

He confided that at home every Friday night you went to the pub and had a few drinks, which were followed by a fight where you might knock a tooth or two out, but you would then have a laugh about it over another drink. But here in Australia when a fight broke out, they called the police! A culture that limited good clean fun was beyond Stretch's powers of adaptation. He was on the plane home within the week.

Divorce, remarriage and the law

⌒

All along, I had entertained some qualms concerning the mix of a law office in a church building. It did cause a clash of paradigms. These came to a head when I was asked to perform the wedding of a woman whose divorce I had handled. I must confess to some misgivings when she said, 'You were so good at my divorce I just knew you would be splendid doing my wedding.' Was I trying too hard? I have no doubt that, where there is an icy destructiveness in a marriage, it is best to move to termination. But every death of a marriage is a blow to our ideal that committed human love can free us to change and conquer our own demons and personal problems.

I have spent a fair part of my legal life appearing in the family court. So every wedding I officiate over is against the backdrop of the matrimonial cases I have done. Matching and dispatching human love is as raw as it gets. Unlike other legal cases that involve fighting a third party over a lease, a personal injury or bent car fender, family law contests for children or property are waged against those whom once were intimately loved. The emotions are so exposed.

I have no doubt that the Family Law Act is a humane piece of legislation. It allows the Court to remove painlessly the legal shell of an empty marriage, with dignity and without messy legal accusation. Its 'no fault' provision for divorce rightly assesses the impossibility of addressing marital wrongs in a court of law. How does a judge assess moral culpability in a matter as personally complex and intertwined as a love relationship? But I also have no doubt that the ease of legal dissolution—twelve months' separation is the only evidence required to obtain a divorce—from entrapment in a marriage has become an opportunity for overturning marriages that may be retrievable. Freedoms provide a razor-sharp, double-edged sword.

I have noticed unsubtle shifts in attitudes toward marriage in the premarital counselling which I've done in the last few years. In the face of deafening cultural claims that marriage and lifelong commitment are too much to expect, I find couples need considerable stiffening to the proposition that life has seasons and it is more gutsy to see them through than abandon the journey. I believe that there is an age of innocent first love that invariably ends, and frankly must end for a deeper love to grow. The psycho-sexual romantic stage of infatuation cannot endure more than twelve to eighteen months. There is commonly a desert or prolonged dull patch that follows the termination of the first innocence, but it can be passed through in the faith that there will be a second innocence, less idealistic but as fulfilling as the first. In the second innocence, there is a wisdom of hindsight which sees that the other person was not necessarily the problem to be resolved by being given the marital flick. More probably, it was the restlessness of life-stage transition and heart hunger, which needed the steadiness of commitment to face painful personal growth before love could be found to be there again in a deeper, richer way.

Too many people fail to negotiate the difficult passages, like the sleep-deprived, hands-on years with young children, the turmoil of mid-life, or the empty-nest crisis. Absolute freedom and personal happiness, the idols in our culture, insinuate that we need not be trapped by vows of commitment belonging to an earlier epoch when we were more settled and somehow different.

I say to all couples in counselling that my prayer is that they will grow old together. I do pray for them. Hopefully, when the stress of the long days' battles are behind them, then the mellowing stage of life in its memory and richness can be shared with a life partner. Work in the Family Court has amply proved to me that there is always going to be someone who appears more attractive, more compatible and perhaps more sexy than your spouse, and that is true whether you are on your first or fifth partner. Swapping the passengers doesn't change the scenery. I firmly believe that marriage provides a foundation for love and is the basis of love as much as the reverse and more accepted notion that love is the basis of marriage.

What a shock the 1994 US studies were to the sexuality mindbenders. They revealed that, contrary to the Hollywood image of rampant extra-marital excesses throughout the culture, eighty-five per cent of married men were faithful to their wives. Even more iconoclastic for the idols of permissiveness was the finding that married men and women had more sex and better sex lives than the unmarried. These statistics conflate with what we have known for some time: that health and longevity of life point to the importance of marriage as a cornerstone. This makes the Family Court a health hazard to be avoided if at all possible.

Judgment, mercy and the law

～

The extremities of life are played out in the courts. It is hard not to see some symbolic prefiguring of the great divine court revealing a true cosmic reordering on judgment day. Human justice is always imperfect because we do not ever know all the facts. God's justice is reckoned to be perfect because all the evidence of history will be on the table.

The most oft-asked question fired at all lawyers is: how can you defend a person whom you know is guilty? Monstrous decisions like the Rodney King case in Los Angeles complicate the public trust in lawyers. We all watched the white police land fifty-five truncheon blows on the head and back of a prostrate black man. But the police lawyers took the jury though the video evidence and convinced them that the police were helpless and Rodney King, though defenceless and beaten to a pulp, was in control of the police and stage-managing the whole violent exercise. The absurd not-guilty verdict led to riots where sixty people died.

The answer to defending the guilty lies in whose job it is to determine guilt. I'm sure the lawyers for the Guildford Four, wrongfully convicted of murder in Britain, were sure their clients were guilty. They were exonerated fourteen years later and the English faith in justice was seismically shaken. A person is not guilty until they are found guilty by a judge who has heard both sides.

I remember my father often saying to me and my brother, 'I do not care who is right or wrong; I am going to punish you both.' As a parent, I now fully understand that it was borne of the weariness involved in adjudicating endless sibling disputes. But back then, that always struck me as flagrantly unfair and—who knows?—it may have been the catalyst that pushed me into studying law. Human justice must hear both sides and refrain from judgment until both are fully aired. A defence counsel with a client who has pleaded not guilty is simply saying the client is exercising their right to insist that the prosecution proves their guilt.

Such are the enormous resources of the State that, when arraigned against the solitary individual, they can dreadfully oppress. Consequently, we have a rule about being innocent until proven guilty and the burden of proof falling on the police. In essence, this is a philosophical decision to say that it is better that some guilty people claim the benefit of the doubt from a not-guilty plea and walk free than some innocent people be wrongfully convicted through having to prove their innocence. I certainly prefer allowing the benefit of the doubt and am happy to represent people pleading not guilty, even though I may entertain my private suspicions.

This bias reflects my suspicion that, at the end of the day, few guilty people truly get way with their crimes. Even if they do, in any event mercy is more important to me than punishment, which rarely delivers either retribution, rehabilitation or deterrence. Prosecuting is necessary, as society has a clear duty to protect itself, but I am glad not to do it myself.

My sixteenth-century Anabaptist forefathers had a strong tradition of pacifism and refused to take up arms or to become magistrates, because it meant exercising the sword in a society that practised capital punishment as a sanction. Their refusal to be the instruments of the State's wrath in legal punishment was a statement that life is always preferable to death, and mercy to judgment. Plenty of others were eager to wear the black cap and pronounce the final words of sentence to the condemned. But their witness chose to model pacifism as an alternative ethic, pointing to a world where grace was stronger than law. Quixotic though it may seem, the dynamic of leaving judgment ultimately to God is the one I prefer.

Punishment, rehabilitation and the law

~

The criminal courts have often become the setting for battles that should have been fought elsewhere. 'Frank' was a case in point. He had spent a year at Machaseh House and was a regular member of the church community. Frank's mum had been very caring and her poverty led her into part-time prostitution. His father was a heavy drinker whose terrifying drunken rages usually left Mum bruised and battered. Frank would lie in bed praying to Jesus to stop the bashing, but it did not stop. A couple of times, he intervened to protect Mum and was beaten black and blue, too. His prayers were sort of answered when Dad left home while Frank was still in primary school.

Mum left home and took a flat in Elwood, near St Kilda. She had a series of lovers, some paying for the favours. Frank particularly remembered a couple of police who would come together and stay playing cards, after giving him money to go and buy a hamburger. One guy who stank of scotch usually brought chocolate for them, but proceeded to callously molest his younger sister.

Frank got into trouble as a young teenager and Mum kicked him out at fourteen. He worked at Luna Park and lived on dope and cold pizza. His big break came when he took a job as a psychiatric nurses' aide and started making a future for himself. Tragically, after some months of depression, he had his first breakdown at twenty-one. He spent four months in one of Melbourne's major psychiatric hospitals. Since then, he has spent a short time every year in hospital.

The way Frank escaped from his mental horror was by taking up a pseudonym borrowed from a triple-certificate nurse he fell in love with, who was disbarred from working because of heroin use. Calling himself by this new name, he would escape into a surreal world of the CIA, who were after him because he was on assignments from the Hell's Angels, depositing millions in personal bank accounts. Many a time I received a phone call from him at 3.00 am to say surreptitiously that the transaction was done and I was now a rich man.

Regrettably, my bank balance looked the same in the cold morning light. Different-coloured taxis passing by Frank were code for different messages, communicated to him from high-ranking CIA colonels. It all made complete sense to him.

It was during one of these psychotic stages that Frank rang me to say he had robbed the local pharmacy and he wanted me to take him to the police station. I was shocked because, bizarre as his world had become, he had never committed a crime. I rang St Kilda police who said that the chemist had been robbed at knife point a few hours before. Frank had been unable to get hospitalised and had taken matters into his own hands. He had walked out with three hundred dollars and given half to the Salvation Army and the rest to a street woman hanging out for some heroin.

On the way to the police station I explained that I could not stay for the whole record of interview, but was there to make sure that Frank let them know he was off his medication and in need of help. I was a little shocked to get the record of interview back and discover that the police had asked him why he had owned up. Frank's response was that he was a Christian who knew right from wrong and that he knew it was wrong. The police asked him if Mr Costello had told him to say that. No, he said, Mr Costello told him to make up 'a bullshit story' that he was crazy.

I had to live with that record of interview as his defence lawyer when the matter came on for trial. He refused bail because he wanted hospitalisation and knew he would get into the psychiatric wing at the metropolitan prison. Fortunately, the judge understood the nature of his debilitating illness and gave him a wholly suspended prison sentence.

Regrettably, mercy and not judgment was going to be needed in large doses at least once again in Frank's case. A year later, I saw the same worrying symptoms and bundled him into a taxi to get him to hospital. We had already unsuccessfully tried to get the local outreach psychiatric teams to visit him, but they were too overwhelmed with requests. I rang the hospital to impress on them his desperation and need of a bed—to no avail, as he came back in the same taxi. The vicious cost-cutting of the State Government had meant no emergency beds.

The next day, he took a knife from the House of Hope and held up a supermart. After initially running away, he calmly walked back with all the money in hand and asked them to call the police. I appeared as a witness rather than as defence counsel this time. Despite the clear evidence of illness and mean-fisted health policies, it was his second armed robbery within a year and a frightening pattern was emerging. It gave the County Court judge a difficult dilemma and she remanded him in custody overnight to think carefully.

The next day, she exercised mercy with another suspended prison sentence, even though it was an extraordinary and highly unusual sentence, given he had breached the existing one. Mercy had triumphed over punishment, a risky precedent in the face of growing public revulsion of violence that demanded judges impose stiffer punishments.

The poor, the rich and the law

～

As I defended many kids on shoplifting charges, I started to think about the discouraging frequency with which I would hear non-illuminating, monosyllabic grunts to my enquiries as to why they had stolen. It is easy to run a plea in mitigation on the basis that this is the child of a single parent from a stressed and unhappy family, all compounded by little encouragement at school that resulted in his falling in with the wrong company. These pleas are so uniform as to write themselves and not warrant any rewriting for the next client.

But often they do not adequately explain the crime. I realised that there were other perpetrators never named on the summons. They were the mindbenders who poured the latest psychological insights into state-of-the-art advertisements. They fashioned glorious propaganda from expensive top-drawer 'market research' into the peer trends. Adolescents in a society that has idolised Madonna looks, Coca Cola drinks, Nike footwear and images of the sleekest and coolest dudes are terribly vulnerable. If your peer group decreed Reebok, then it had the authority of an *ex cathedra* pontifical command. You tore your jeans along the right crease and then bought or stole your Reeboks, otherwise you felt like social cactus.

Now for the really poor, of whom we have many already, with their numbers growing, everything they see is something they cannot afford. You walk into a department store which sensually exposes the very item your peer group wears and your mother says the family cannot afford. The store design invites you with a seductive self-serve to handle and try on. It reminds you that all the alive, cool humans you desperately want to impress and belong to possess these.

Little wonder you conceal it under a jumper and make a run for your very identity. Marketing psychology has some culpability in overpowering your will—but try and run that as a defence to shoplifting in our courts. Consumerism is for those who can play the game and it's hardball for the losers, who are often poor.

Morality and the law
⌒

What makes a thing illegal? Legislation that proscribes acts is based upon social beliefs about right and wrong. But in a relativist age, the notion of right and wrong is a moveable feast. Why is a thing right now when it used to be so wrong? A man now in his sixties who attended our church for a period asked me just that question. He went to prison in the early 1960s for two years for the offence of buggery and felt at the time that he had done wrong and deserved to be punished. Now he doesn't, so what has changed?

Right and wrong is different to good and evil. The latter is made of more absolute fibre and is less partial to fashions in morality. The present Pope keeps preaching the difference and it brings to mind Graham Greene's famous observation that Protestants believe in right and wrong, but Catholics in good and evil. The former is an ethical standard that can be debated, modified and changed. The category of evil can only be confessed, absolved and forgiven by the power of salvation that comes from outside. It is of deeper stain than wrong, and is irremediable.

But the two are difficult to distinguish. Murder is evil, but not wrong if performed by the State in capital punishment or in time of war. Theft is evil, but not wrong if lands are won by a military invasion, such as Indonesia annexing East Timor and leaving its sea oil intact for a trade treaty, granting a windfall to Australia. It is not theft if it is for the good of the economy.

Law follows social ethics but usually with the speed of a man with a ball and chain affixed to his legs. The speed is increasing, thanks to the vaporisation of serious ethical debate in the face of economic hegemony. When those whose lives are based on the absolutes of the ten commandments discover that these absolutes are as defenceless and susceptible to the prevailing social mores of personal and national greed, then it causes considerable confusion, anger and insecurity.

These citizens understood that gaming was a part of a police department known as the Vice and Gaming Squad because it was an evil to be prosecuted. It comes as a breath-taking denouement to have the State sponsor gaming as a civilised recreation, and even more of a shock to hear the Victorian Premier launch the Melbourne casino saying this 'represented the new spirit of Victoria', the future vision for the State. This debauched statesmanship laughed off empirical evidence about the hideous addictions and corruptive processes that might accompany a spanking new gambling house. The Premier pointed to the bulging State coffers and promise of extra revenue from attracting high-flying, high-rolling gamblers and lots of locals. These could subsidise a few therapies for gambling addicts.

That which was once illegal and belonged to the pigeon-hole of vice is elevated to the level of a political achievement of moral proportions. The transfer of income in gambling from the poor to the rich and to the government is well-documented. Of course, the Premier claimed a popular mandate, but one fears that if an opinion poll declared a majority in favour of State-sponsored paedophilia because of the revenue it might generate from international paedophiles, then on the same basis they might enjoy protection. It would be right at law. Right and wrong have swapped their black-and-white hats and the sheriff does not know who to chase any more.

The very week the Crown Casino opened coincided with my tenure at the House of Hope. I faced ashen-faced friends who had blown all their savings, asking me to manage their whole earnings or dole cheque, as they had fallen for the State's lies that the casino was a place of roaring fun. The casino was opened to fix up the empty State treasury; the House of Hope—and other such community agencies—was left to deal with the resultant broken lives: direct cause and effect.

Gambling was attacked last century by the Christian Women's Temperance Movement. They saw its destructiveness to family life and campaigned powerfully, earning the title of wowser ('We Only Want Social Evils Remedied'). They had an uphill fight because gambling plugged into the democratic mateship myth. The Melbourne Cup was the only democratic race in the world, with all the horses being handicapped to equalise them—a practice unheard of elsewhere. Gentry and lower classes all liked a flutter, breaking down social boundaries. But gambling had been regarded by the State as a regrettable but inevitable back-door activity. Now it is regarded as a legitimate, even praiseworthy, front-door virtue.

The lady holding the scales of justice is blindfolded to remind us that the law is utterly impartial. Sometimes the law is simply blind and cannot recognise morality when hit in the face by it.

One of my clients was a working-class teenager who did an armed robbery with a sawn-off shotgun. He and his girlfriend bought some heroin with the proceeds and blew the rest of the money on a motel. She was apprehended and confessed to doing the whole job. My client subsequently experienced a Christian conversion and, after some deep thought, decided to give himself up, even though the police were satisfied that the woman had done the whole job alone.

I turned up in the County Court faced with an unusual task. I had to prove to the judge and the police that my client was guilty. They did not want to know about it and the prosecutor admitted to some embarrassment at having two defendants when he only wanted one.

I won the case, successfully proving to the court that my client was guilty. He had held up the store while his girlfriend had simply driven the getaway car. The court was all at sea in trying to punish someone whose morality did not square with the quick, efficient administration of justice. He, too, was given a suspended sentence—after the judge commented on how this was for him, in his long career on the bench, a most surprising case.

To be present in the moments of acute fear and be able to offer advocacy was an extension of my ministry. The crisis of a legal problem was often the moment of self-insight that opened up new possibilities for grace and transformation.

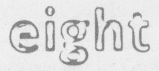

Politicking on behalf
of the powerless

In August 1993 I was elected Mayor of the City of St Kilda. It was to be a poisoned chalice and I was to fall short of seeing my mayoral term out by six weeks—the victim of a local government restructuring that saw the St Kilda municipality abolished, the first in the abolition of every single one of Victoria's 205 municipalities, which were replaced with hand-picked representatives of the Premier.

I was to be the last of St Kilda's mayors, and presided over the wake that mourned the death of 137 years of municipal history and self-government. But on becoming mayor, I and most other councillors were unaware or unwilling to accept that we were in the 'last days', and I looked upon my term with enthusiasm to nourish the community that I had come to love.

My entry into local politics was haphazard, a chain of events and opportunities converging at a time when I was ripe for further challenge. But I guess, having a father who taught politics for thirty-three years, it was on the agenda as he had helped engender within me an interest, bordering on an obsession, with politics in all its forms.

Most families had a golden rule for domestic harmony: no

open discussion of the divisive subjects of politics or religion. Yet these were the topics that formed the lifeblood of my family's discourse. Few meal times passed without us heatedly discussing the latest political occurrence, or teasing out the implications of the last sermon we had heard. Of course, sport made up the essential third element of domestic debate but, despite earnest attempts, none of us was capable of making our living in sport. This was not, however, the case with politics or religion, to which at least Peter and I turned our professional lives. Our familial grounding had shaped us well.

By 1991 it was clear that in my brother Peter the family had already gained one career politician and that was considered plenty. My sister, Janet, in the teaching profession and me in the Church (or was that in the law?—well, whatever) was regarded as a complementary balance. The family script had not anticipated any more politicians. Peter and I had both pursued public roles. Peter is a national leader, and although his path is different to mine the commitment to changing society and facilitating justice is a shared one.

The evolution of my entry into the political domain grew out of my pastoral work among the homeless, who inconveniently kept turning up on our church doorstep. I found myself in the mid-1980s investing generous amounts of my pastoral time trying to find a bed for St Kilda residents who had been forced out and were without shelter.

The political climate in St Kilda in the early 1990s

⤙

This was the peak of the housing crisis, when St Kilda was seriously discovered by the yuppies who had formerly shied away from sleaze city. It was only going to be a matter of time before its location—five kilometres from the central business district, glorious views of Port Philip Bay and proximity to Melbourne's best restaurants and theatres—would spark a glint in the eyes of the new gentry.

So in the eighties, exactly a century after the first land boomers built palatial St Kilda, open season was declared for new boomers and gentrification. Hordes of 'new money' starters snaffled up the former mansions—now bedsits for thousands of poor—to restore them as single-family dwellings. A new class gobbled down the single-fronted workmen's cottages, splashing them with heritage colours, throwing up picket fences, ripping out floral carpet, lino, 1950s kitchens and briquette heaters, and installing polished board floors, granite kitchen bench tops, open fireplaces and central heating. Even the hellish 1960s cream-brick walk-up flats started to get the treatment. They would receive a new legal identity known as a strata title and a wondrous set of smart clothes via a quick paint job. Tizzy wrought-iron balconies and crisp sunblinds brazenly adorned the exteriors and hid a myriad of internal crises.

This was wonderful for those professionals or investors, but unwanted disaster for poor tenants whose low rents had long reflected St Kilda's undesirable postcode. The Ritz Hotel, opposite the House of Hope, was a sleazy strip joint when we moved there a decade ago, but in the last few years had become an upmarket restaurant and dressy night spot for under-28s.

The open market has no nostalgic sentiment for city loyalty or long-staying battlers. No matter how many generations of their families had lived here, this was representing progress. They must not stifle the cultural expression of reclaiming the slums and reception areas for migrants. Vibrant inner-city living was now the go.

In the church and in the legal office we saw many casualties. Tenants arriving at our legal office forlornly asked if they had any legal defence to the dreaded notice to quit that evinced no sympathy for long and faithful tenure. The answer was always no. Others who came were traditional boarding-house renters, ex-psychiatric patients and others who had drifted to the inner city and carried its secrets, its culture and its magic. Many had lived in the former mansions, by now rabbit warrens of flatettes and bedsits, for thirty or more years. The owners of these boarding houses, along with a number of the proprietors of the cheap private hotels, were now selling up. Solid community services were likely to become obsolescent as more and more were pushed out. Setting up those services elsewhere would be enormously expensive.

The pressure of locating alternative housing in St Kilda for those who asked our help became unrelenting. It consumed much of our pastoral time and I realised I was reeling from dealing with crisis to crisis. There had to be some macro-solutions. In early 1991 I did some research and co-authored a book on planning legislation and affordable housing. I discovered to my shock how sparse the public housing levels were in St Kilda when we had huge numbers of pensioners, ill people, homeless youth and unemployed in the city.

It was then that I linked up with a remarkable bunch of non-party political residents. These had formed a neighbourhood electoral group to contest elections and wrest control of council from the developers, estate agents and fellow travellers who had dominated it for decades. Atrocious planning decisions were embracing the developers' dream and the residents' nightmare. This developer dominated. Council had welcomed the prospect of a huge marina in St Kilda harbour that would have berthed fabulous boats, the playthings of the rich and famous, but limited the use of the beach for swimming, strolling and sand-castles. Developers had also applied to build high towers of offices and flats along the foreshore that threatened to make St Kilda the southern cousin of Queensland's Gold Coast.

This group of local independents decided to say no. Their chosen name was 'Turn the Tide'. It was to turn the strong tide against the harbour marina and the uncontrolled high-rise development, by introducing maximum height controls along the St Kilda foreshore and challenging the loss of the character of this place as a refuge for the poor. It proposed a council-funded and public-sponsored affordable housing program. These were highly interventionist policies and, to some citizens, way beyond the charter of councils that were normally preoccupied with roads, rates and rubbish. But in 'Turn the Tide', a resilient pride in the streetscape and interfacing with the social mix united the horizons of a band of committed residents.

Normally, such proposals would die within nano-seconds after being uttered, or be humoured as colourful rhetoric not to be taken seriously by responsible business-minded rate-payers. But a seismic shift in local politics had recently occurred. The voting roll, which had included only resident or absent ratepayers, had been thrown open in the 1980s to all residents. This gave tenants a vote in the city in which they resided. For St Kilda, with its huge percentage of tenants, this was an electoral hand-grenade. 'Turn the Tide' initiatives were attractive to tenants and to community-minded ratepayers. This meant a new force was emerging with the potential to win power.

By 1988 this remarkable group, who had no party structure or backing funds, had won power in a city of over 45 000 people. It had waved goodbye to the marina, seen off the grandiose foreshore developments with a planning amendment introducing height regulation and, most radically, entered into a five-year joint-housing agreement with the State government and Federal government to spend fifteen million dollars on affordable public housing in St Kilda.

The decision to contest the St Kilda elections

The new local ferment opened up radical possibilities to achieve my goals of justice, fairness and harmony in a local community. I decided to run as a candidate and with others, developed a platform that addressed the central issue of my ministry in St Kilda. Elections soon revolved around the major issue of committing ratepayers' dollars to housing, which was traditionally a State Government responsibility. Other general political issues supported by Turn the Tide included funding of the arts, generous assistance to community groups, protecting the environment from headlong development, encouraging bike and public transport over cars, and balancing the needs of an intense residential community with the huge influx of tourists each weekend. Simply put, it represented a political divide that ran through most of the politics of the 1980s: what was the proper public realm for government intervention and a public sector in the face of an all-conquering fashion known as privatisation?

I took my decision to run for council before the church congregation. There had been some unhappy historical episodes of the clergy meddling in temporal affairs and compromising the task of ministry. Indeed, strict Anabaptists, the sixteenth-century European forbears of the Baptist movement, would never contemplate a political position. The United States had thrown up some prominent Baptist leaders, like Jimmy Carter, Martin Luther King and Jesse Jackson, but the tradition in Australia was largely pious and private. Baptists mainly felt they were Liberal voters, as they saw themselves reflected in the frugal, hard-working, clean-living, middle-class values captured by former Prime Minister Menzies in his appeal to the 'forgotten people'.

Church meetings in a Baptist tradition are thoroughly democratic and, for that reason, thoroughly worrying to the minister. The local congregation is totally sovereign in hiring and firing its ministers and setting policy and direction. No bishop can overrule, no denominational leader can pull rank. The congregation has total control and it votes at quarterly church meetings on all issues affecting its communal life. The best instincts maximise participation; the worst maximise domination by an articulate and powerful minority.

Thankfully, the St Kilda Church had developed from about fifteen voting members when Merridie and I came to over ninety in 1991, and they carried the motto of 'a community committed at the core and open at the edges' in their hearts and not just on the letterhead. They voted nearly unanimously to allow me to run, and promised their prayerful support even if they individually could not agree with me on every issue. I was to continue working as Minister and Lawyer during my time on St Kilda Council.

I remember only one member of the congregation not being at all enamoured of my stand. Coincidentally, he was an estate agent a little worried by my advocacy of public housing. Election day came and there were four other candidates contesting the one position for my ward. After a long day talking to people at the polling booths, I planned to be at the Town Hall, the biggest booth in my ward, for the last two hours from 4.00 pm to the close of polls at 6.00 pm.

When I arrived to shake hands and relieve the person handing out my how-to-vote cards, I saw this estate agent standing nearby, distributing my campaign literature. I felt quite moved by this generous gesture and asked him what he was doing there. He smiled and said, 'I do not believe in your politics, but I believe in you!' With that sort of support, I won convincingly. Whilst closely linked with the 'Turn the Tide' group, I had chosen to stand as an independent. I felt this gave me greater freedom to express my conscience and remain true to my core values.

Adjusting to life as mayor

So I entered the fray from August 1991. Eva, my parishioner living in the Regal Hotel, came to my induction as a councillor. I will never forget her sweeping up handfuls of sandwiches at the supper which followed. She told me they were to feed the residents of the Regal Hotel and I knew I had been elected to keep poor but deeply caring individuals like Eva in affordable housing.

As she walked past the newly installed mayor, looking resplendent in his robe and chains, I heard her say, 'Congratulations, love, you look terrific in that dress.' Even mayors can be lost for words.

I quickly got used to a total rearrangement of my schedule, with meetings dotted throughout the week, and a thick blue plastic satchel delivered every Tuesday and Friday evenings with papers for my deliberation. It added a new meaning to the word 'busy' for me personally and also for us as a family. We were all on a giant learning curve, in terms of coping with the hours, the requests, the expectations. The numerous committees all threw up for me a new language and process that had to be absorbed.

It also proved a big adjustment for the family. I was out almost every night of the week, and most council meetings precluded an evening meal at home. It plunged us into stresses we had never experienced before. The main consolation was that I was working locally. We also had to adjust to a mobile phone—truly a blessing and a curse.

I quickly learnt that being a politician is a world apart from the political observer's role that had consumed my life up to that point. The difficulties of nailing my colours to the mast became quickly apparent. Politicians prefer to keep their options open and hold firmly to as few positions as possible. You just never know when that strong statement and unconditional commitment is going to boomerang viciously back on you.

An embarrassing lesson in this regard came with a front-page colour picture of me as mayor in my business-suit, standing barefoot on the beach assuring everyone that the bay was free from all pollutants and health-hazardous *E. coli*, and totally safe to swim in that summer. Within a week, Melbourne was deluged by torrential rain, causing the collapse of a major drainage system, which poured its effluent into the bay. Up went the signs right along the inner-city beaches: 'Unsafe for Swimming'. I ceased to make enthusiastic mayoral encyclicals.

On the other hand, I tried to avoid the hedging that makes voters so cynical about politicians. The democratic system only works if clear alternative policies and visions are put up for choice. The fudging and mumbling in order to stay uncommitted for electoral advantage compromises the process. I stood clearly for the St Kilda housing program and found that it raised hostility.

One of my opposing candidates had been a developer who lived outside St Kilda and had extensive interests in the city, as well as in Sydney. He rang me and complained bitterly that some of my colleagues were playing dirty pool in the lead-up to the election by saying untrue things about him. He warned me to stop them or he would get very nasty. I asked him what they were saying and he replied he would not go into it, but just gave me the warning to stop them. I was mystifed and promised to stop whatever it was if he would only tell me.

Eventually, I coaxed out of him his grievance. They were saying he did not live in St Kilda and he believed that this was tarnishing his electoral image. I took a deep breath and said, 'But I understand that this is completely true.' He agreed that it was, but maintained they should not be saying it—and then he immediately hung up. He lost the election and the next I heard of him was when he hit the front page of the local paper for running a boarding house that was condemned as unfit for human habitation.

Privatisation and the public good in local government

⌁

Council meetings were a forum for the competing destinies of St Kilda to be debated and teased out. Planning issues were the hottest political potatoes. The looser coalition of Turn the Tide and independent councillors recognised that our decisions about the physical infrastructure were a lasting legacy to exalt or degrade the streetscape for future generations. Hence, a mixture of boldness, farsightedness and historical conservation was needed.

We sought to prevent the loss of critical housing stock by passing a local law on dilapidated buildings. This required owners to spend money on properties they had deliberately let run down until they had a persuasive argument to demand a demolition order from us. Council had been powerless to arrest the cynical and programmed neglect. After demolition had been justified on safety grounds, a modern building would rise from the ashes. This architectural phoenix would never offer residence for St Kilda's poor, but penthouses and luxury apartments for those with endless options to acquire a roof over their heads. We also tried to encourage developers to pay a housing levy for the replacement of affordable housing if their development proposal obliterated such stock. Whilst it sometimes worked— we achieved some important breakthroughs—we knew that we were testing the limits of state legislation.

Behind these rather intrusive planning interventions was an ethical and cultural stance. Planning law is necessarily interventionist, as zoning determines the social uses of land. Large sums of money are contingent upon such zoning choices, and open space and proper planning is vital to residential amenity. Land is subject to societal constraints and the owner is never absolutely free to exploit it. As the prime resource in a city, it is a valuable commodity for the community, residents and private speculators. Balancing the conflicting interests is sensitive work. Harnessing the profit motives of developers to employ their private capital to build houses and factories, but maintaining the community interest that must subsidise the infrastructure for water, electricity, gas, sewerage and other services, requires fine tuning.

The majority of us on council believed that on ethical grounds St Kilda should retain affordable housing for the poor. Justice is not always a recognisable criterion for planning decisions, but I am proud to say it got a window seat in our council. Furthermore, on cultural grounds we asserted that the mix of social and economic groups was important for the vibrancy and vitality of the city. If yuppiedom totally won, then a bland cultural sterilisation would result.

We needed ethical arguments because the economic ones were at best uncertain. There was no doubt that it was cheaper to build affordable housing on the outskirts of Melbourne where the land was less expensive: more 'bang' for the public buck. But on the outskirts of the city, the public transport and community services were still undeveloped and there were great distances to travel to free recreation, like the beaches, over our long, hot summers. At least in St Kilda there was fantastic public transport and loads of community supports and stimulation. Like Third World cities where the poor camp is on the edge, and in squalor without services, we threatened that fate for our poor if they were forced out of the inner-city suburbs. A pastor friend of mine who works in one of Melbourne's fast-burgeoning outer suburbs told me few of the poor want to be there. Many cannot afford cars and so are miserably isolated.

Council represented a forum where such civic discourse that shaped the social and physical realities of our place, our suburb and our lives could occur. Civic discourse is an endangered dialogue. It takes hours of unpaid work to be on council and a great deal of commitment by one's family or partner. Historically those who do put up their hands are regarded with suspicion. Is it a political career they want, or some business advantage by being on the ground floor of decision making?

Perhaps a local profile as a councillor is their way of advertising their product.

I was surprised at the prevalence of this view. When I was in the forefront of media attention at the height of the debate about local government reform, journalists would ask every week what the next step was for me. Was it State or Federal politics? It was off their map that I had no further political ambitions and might just believe in the issues for their own sake.

I found that this was largely true of my colleagues. A generation earlier, St Kilda councillors may have had political careers that sailed too close to business interests, but the calibre of councillors in my time, their hard work and vigorous debate, was exceptionally high. Tribute needs to be paid to civic-mindedness because it is a diminishing resource. I discovered that it abounded in our area and in other councils around the state. The petty aspersions cast so glibly on unpaid local councillors may be yet another manifestation of our national pastime of cutting down any poppy with a modicum of height, and devaluing an important source of social capital.

A forum for articulation of competing visions for one's city is a great gift. The dissolving of local councils over 1994 and the promised future return of them to us as large, amalgamated entities has focussed on the argument of efficiency. This has been at the huge price of local story. Its loss is keenly felt in a technological world moving from broadcasting to narrowcasting. This means that the forums to toss around the multi-myths of a pluralistic society are dramatically reduced. A common culture that chanced its arm on a common story through the wide net of broadcasting is losing the influence of that medium. It may be at times an underfed and impoverished common culture, but at least the main debates have still been sustained.

Privatisation and the public good in State and Federal politics

～

These concerns deserve serious debate. At federal level, we have two parties desperately crowing about their distinctions when they seem indistinguishable to most Australians. Privatisation and the use of the market to provide public services and utilities is the catchcry of both parties, and the great debate of the moment centres on the speed of the disposal. Any buyer, experience not necessarily needed, will do. Why? Because the dogma is ascendant that private enterprise gives more for less and the public sector stuffs it up.

Convince the public of that after the scandal of watching private entrepreneurs and private banks dissipating wealth with crazy borrowing and spectacular crashes through the 1980s. As one trade union leader wryly noted, the privatising of prisons will create a world first as our fallen tycoons are gaoled in their own prisons. A new twist, surely, on owner-occupied buildings. That is privatisation!

As in clothes, so in politics; fashions that dictate higher or lower hemlines are not rational, despite the boasts of economic rationalism. Years later, the decisions look as foolish the clothes do to the eyes of the fashionable nineties. Of course, we are patronised with the explanation that the science of economics has rationally directed each decision to dismantle more public areas.

If any voices of opposition to this orthodoxy are raised, then economists bark sharply with all the viciousness of tormented spaniels. Most of them fly off like Mary Poppins and can never be found when their computer-driven economic models and sophisticated theories fail. We heard their assured pontifications and now know they were but the latest fashion.

The commonsense punters who have turned a detached eye towards these fashions are starting to believe that predictive economics is no more scientific than examining the entrails of a sheep—except that perhaps the entrails are slightly more accurate.

Between the bookends of economic theorists are lots of public-sector and local council jobs being sacrificed as too costly. Private enterprise is still unequivocally applauded. The myth proclaims that this sector is the real creator of wealth, whereas public service creates nothing. This fashion forgets its limits. Private wealth can only be created out of resources that belong to everyone because they first belong to God. The Hebrew scriptures assert that the earth is the Lord's and the fullness thereof. If it is God's world gifted to us, then it comes with an obligation of stewardship in its cultivation for the benefit of all. It is an obscenity to award it to the private profiteers. Every dollar created comes from within the social circle of a public infrastructure quarried out by a communal ethic.

Many Christians are idolatrously sucked into the doctrine of privatisation. At the back of their minds, they have a God made in the image of a captain of industry loved by individualistic capitalism. He is a strong, sovereign individual who proprietorially owns and disposes of anything and everything. Little wonder they act with the same individualism. But the Christian God is revealed as triune, a community of three persons whose interdependence is so marked that this God is monotheistically confessed to be one. This is not an arbitrary individual authorising us to act according to our own profit instincts, but a community of persons serving alongside us and empowering us to serve others. Jesus Christ epitomised such service of all.

Part of the confusion is the belief that a personal God is the same as an individualistic God. I believe in a personal God who has shown us his face in Jesus of Nazareth. I believe in a God who hears a tree fall in the dead of night in a forest and sees the sparrow who falls from the sky. Personal, yes, but a self-contained, rugged, privatised and individualistic God, no.

Is privatisation not going to channel the fallen self-interest that original sin has deposited in the human heart? Maybe, but it must be kept in check. It is the same human nature at work, in private enterprise or in the public sector. Keeping the two domains in healthy tension is probably the best safeguard for accountability and productivity. Australia is one of the oldest democracies in the world. We led the world in gaining the first 48-hour week for workers. We were one of the first societies to give women the vote. We even had the first socialist government in the world (in Queensland in the 1890s). We were one of the first countries to offer universal primary school education as an expression of our egalitarian 'fair go' for all beliefs. Why should we not try to be the social laboratory in justice again?

Imagine if we agreed that ever higher living standards are not the prime goal of our national economic policy; that governments be directed by us to create jobs and stop regarding a permanent level of unemployment as inevitable—even more, beneficial for a competitive economy. That is never said bluntly, but our leaders certainly whisper about the unemployed as the necessary collateral damage for a healthy economy.

Imagine a social contract that declared it immoral for eight per cent of the population and a much higher number of youths to be treated as sacrificial unemployed lambs on the altar of growth. Imagine a national conversation that displayed enough candour and refreshing honesty to admit that there are not enough jobs for all who want meaningful work in our society, so we will organise justly and encourage part-time work and job-sharing to avoid adulating the winners and scapegoating the losers. A reason for true national pride might surface. Out of our tradition of egalitarianism we could be the first country to replace the All Ordinaries Index, which so dominates our television news, with the *social* index on our news services each night. This would register the number of trees planted that day, the number of homeless still to be housed, how many unemployed were still to find jobs, and how many families were still below the poverty line.

I have never understood the sickness of soul that suggests we cannot raise taxes to pay for a future for our kids because it would kill off the incentive of the money movers. When we have one of the lowest tax regimes in the OECD, why *wouldn't* our business leaders say they are proud to contribute because it will leaven the poverty of others? If social selflessness of this kind was as lauded as business success we might take one small step for us and one big step for humankind.

St Kilda's multicultural community

⤙

One of my favourite duties as mayor was to preside at citizenship ceremonies. Families and friends would flock in for the occasion. We had one each month, with approximately seventy people dressed in their finery to become Australians. Pictures with the mayor in his robes and perched on his mayoral throne always followed. As I presented a citizenship certificate and a gum tree to our newest citizens, I had cause to reflect on how Mohammed, Svetlana and Nguyen felt about swearing allegiance to Queen Elizabeth II in order to prove they were loyal Aussies. If ever there was a moment that moved me to republicanism, it was the bizarreness of these migrants who had no ties with Britain stumbling through this solemn oath of allegiance to a foreign head of Australia. History and continuity with the past is important, but so is embracing a rapidly changing world.

Symbols exist to unify. But when the symbols divide more than they unify, as appears to be the case with the royal family, then they need to be reconstructed or abandoned. It is hard to believe that Prince Charles will be able to retrieve a genuine respect for the Crown. People may have secretly known that the royals were a pretty ordinary family given bundles of money and told to unify the nation as its titular head. But the mystery of the Crown is now completely demystified, thanks to a thorough media exposure of the morals of Prince Charles and the failed relationships of his siblings; their ordinariness has slipped below normal standards of the ordinary.

The days of the House of Windsor as a symbol that unites Australians are seriously numbered. But in a multi-myth environment, replacing this with another symbol is a tall order.

My speech at citizenship ceremonies usually took up themes of Australia's achievements in building a multicultural society at a time when many other European societies were atrophying, or embracing vicious tribal versions of blood-and-soil patriotisms. We had our blind spots, particularly in our treatment of Aborigines, and we still have a long distance to travel to salve our uneasy conscience. The Mabo land rights decision, which overturned the offensive legal notion that Australia was an unoccupied continent and that the English acquired original title, along with the complementary legislation granting land-acquisition funds for Aborigines, applied some balm to that weeping sore.

Nonetheless, I am stoked that the penal colony down under, whose first British settlers were chosen by the 'best judges in England', has made a contribution to the conversation of the nations—by building a tolerant and harmonious society that, after Israel, is proportionally the most multicultural in the world. Without blindly glossing over our blots, I have to say that the fear of the stranger and rigidity of life I experienced in Switzerland seems much less present here.

St Kilda was doing her part in this declaration that refugees and free settlers could all live together as supportive neighbours. Our council, which I had the privilege of chairing, worked assiduously on a strong multicultural policy. Our multicultural festival was a veritable Pentecost of tongues and experiences. Much of this began with the welcoming of new citizens and their cultures along with their loyalty to the new place. We encouraged a sensitive cultivation of all their distinctions and vowed not to risk its erasure with citizenship. Fear of obliteration of the links with their past was a major emotional hurdle for many.

Yes, there were some enormously sensitive decisions. In one of our most visible parks, a group of Koories lit their campfires and drank bottles of cheap sherry. Sadly, as a violated group who often turned their hurt on each other and occasionally on those passing by, they attracted many complaints. Traders were particularly upset because their unkempt, stumbling presence would intimidate customers. It was simple if we played it by the book. Fires were against the by-laws and sleeping out was vagrancy. But this was St Kilda, home to all those groups excommunicated from the civilised world. We understood that a fire was a mainstay of Aboriginal culture, and there had been enough deaths in custody to know that authorising the police to lock them up was not a solution.

One proposal was to insist that alcohol could only be drunk in Fitzroy Street, which is where the particular park is located, if you bought wine at an outdoor cafe. This was the height of white hypocrisy. Effectively, it granted rights to those who could afford the house red, but not to those whose pocket change could only purchase takeaway stubbies. Despite many racist comments, including some from a popular radio identity, we permitted the Aborigines to have their fire and paint a marvellous Aboriginal mural on the adjacent toilet block. Sponsoring a native crafts market and art classes for them was another proactive step. It has not solved the complaints, but St Kilda is still regarded as a place to belong for the poorest and most hurt.

Sadly, after our dismissal, one of the first acts of the commission was to demolish this toilet block. Heresy has no rights in an economic-rationalist council.

The value of local government

A local seat of government is a unifying symbol. The mayor, as first citizen, grants pomp and circumstance to openings and local events that need a profile. The ceremonial side of life that transforms an event into an occasion is vital. Local government attends to the ceremonial nature of life by breathing some transcendence into mundane events and bestowing some dignity and ritual.

As one who is 'low culture' by instinct, it came as a surprise to me to recognise that civility expressed in civicness is a profound need in our cities. I had always thought that the civic world was too precious. Old prints of men in top hats and ladies in full-length skirts at civic gatherings looked faintly ridiculous. Was that not an old Victorian caste system? It reminded me of the secular form of predestination in Melbourne where 'the chosen' have become members of the Melbourne Cricket Club, and the unchosen like me sit in the outer and boo the 'superior' members for scornfully spurning the Mexican wave.

Quirky events like the Angling Ladies' Day, when the men cook up a storm to appease their wives for their frequent truancy from home in the cause of fishing, and more standard events like opening film, music and art festivals, and endless speeches at AGMs of various community groups are community-building. A mayor with an overview of the richly diverse community life helps link so many groups in a common cause of civic pride. I refused to engage in the 'narrowspeak' of economists and politicians, who talked much of council rates, expenditure levels and efficiencies. I deliberately embraced 'broadspeak', choosing topics of hope, love and belonging in civic addresses. So much of our public space is occupied by politicians whose opinion is invited on everything from morals to the meaning of life. Their cautious political narrowspeak is a severe limitation on public discourse.

I remember opening a wing of a Jewish aged home and greeting the listeners with *shalom*. They nodded vigorously and enthusiastically. That magnificent Hebrew word means more than 'hello'. It wraps up personal salvation, community health and justice in its vision of a world where all the colours blend into one. The Hebrew scriptures speak of *shalom* in the courts and in the harvest scales, and of *shalom* in personal relationships. It is a radically alternative vision to the prevailing political mantra of today—applauding winners and shunning losers. *Shalom* asks the question of why there is a widening gap between rich and poor, and, if water and power and seed varieties are all privatised and community broken up, who is going to protect the poor? It asks why, in a world of plenty, so many are still hungry.

We already have a world where transnational companies run by private individuals are more powerful than national governments, and we are selling more of our future to them. Is this not to choose a path in the valley of the shadow of death? We have already patented the food varieties that once were owned in the common domain. Religiously, *shalom* taught us that the earth is the Lord's and given for all. Or, in Bono of U2's immortal words, all committed to *shalom* agree that 'I'm going to kick the darkness till it bleeds daylight. I believe in love.'

The threat to local government in St Kilda

⌁

But there was a brown snake lurking in the long grass. I was a devout believer in small units as the most appropriate for decision making and community building. I regarded big government, big business and big unions as all sharing a common allegiance and editing out the participation of other, smaller and more diverse interests.

Local government had embraced the big-ticket change called 'compulsory competitive tendering'. Competition can bring benefits, like a focus on costs, but these come at a cost, in terms of jobs, and the quality of services. But this was not the end of it. The government went further and announced that all councils would be amalgamated into much bigger units; all councils across Victoria would be summarily dissolved and non-councillors would be appointed indefinitely with the full authority of a council. This was unprecedented anywhere in Australasia; elsewhere, if councils were amalgamated, then elected councillors stayed in power to oversee the transition.

We knew in St Kilda that a smaller community like ours had a better chance of owning decisions such as that to provide affordable housing because it had developed a local culture that was responsive to community. Once amalgamated into a larger unit, residents would be far less likely to empathise with and contribute to community services many kilometres away. Just as a church community can respond to needs because they are known and personal, so a smaller community acts compassionately. A community with such disparate social groups was held together by inclusivity and tolerance. A huge municipality, with no shared history and without knowledge of the local rogues and heroes who give flesh to a small community, would not be capable of this. Yes, there were some efficiencies to be gained in an amalgamation, but there were costs to a cohesive community.

Intriguingly some international studies had found that the most efficient size for councils was approximately 8000 to 10 000 people. France had an average size of 2000 and the US was not much bigger. Efficiencies should be measured not only in output, but in community spirit and participation. England had gone down the route of amalgamation and shut down some wonderful small towns in the process. Funny that we came up with the idea when other nations were growing ambivalent because of its destruction of smaller centres. But the government pressed on with all the cunning of an Amway salesman. It appointed an 'independent board' housed one floor below the government minister's office to consult, but set up predetermined council sizes that must be delivered.

This news brought dismay to many in St Kilda and, rather

than roll over submissively, the council of which I was mayor resolved to fight. Some felt that amalgamation was a justifiable process if it were truly driven by the local community on the basis of clear benefits. However, this was not to be, as the process was a farce. A predetermined size had been agreed to by the government and the council's written submission was ignored. Many in the community felt that this cynical treatment was more destructive than the substantive issue.

St Kilda held some huge public meetings with passions running high to protest its shoddy treatment. Thousands of private submissions poured into the government on St Kilda's behalf. Badges and T-shirts declaring 'St Kilda the eternal city, too good to lose', stencils on footpaths, rallies, concerts, bands, and an outpouring of allegiance to this city's identity followed.

The Jewish community within St Kilda were amongst the most vocal. I received countless letters urging me as the mouthpiece for St Kilda not to waver. They certainly did not believe that the Premier was anti-Semitic, but some did worry at his trammelling of the democratic process. A couple took me aside and quietly and intensely explained that the echoes back to the 1930s were troubling, as one of the first acts of Hitler in Nazi Germany was to sack all the mayors. That certainly helped me gird up my loins.

We knew we could force a referendum if we obtained a petition with ten per cent of our community's signatures within fourteen days. That was an enormous task, but the trojan St Kilda residents went to work and collected 14 000 signatures in the allotted time. We had our referendum and the voice of the city was clear. Ninety per cent of those who voted (which was nearly a third of the city) were against amalgamation. To the shock of so many who had this naive belief in process and democracy, it mattered not a whit. The government simply ignored it as the plans were set in concrete.

Some reflections on St Kilda's loss of its local council

⤳

I was carrying a heavy burden, as many minority groups in St Kilda were feeling insecure. They knew that the council was committed to a public space for them, but they had no idea what a management mentality would bring from a big, bland, new entity that was artificially superimposed on historic cities. Identity was critical to these vulnerable groups and their feeling of identity was tied up with St Kilda's.

I always knew that our battle was that of David against Goliath. The ideology of bigness was the prescriptive fashion. We had no protection under the Australian or Victorian constitutions, which shocked most residents who believed that the third tier of government, and the one closest to the people, had inherent rights.

My concerns were broader. I had entertained beliefs that our consumer culture was organised against history: if a thing was superficially cheaper, then all memory and history were dispensable. I had observed how State Government bureaucracies were impervious to social compassion, social difference and local justice. They liked uniformity, and too many councils with their idiosyncratic ways just got up their noses. This was an epoch when government was an exercise in the cost-accounting style of management. The forces of fragmentation tearing at our soul, our families, and institutions like Church and law, had diabolically infested government. In the absence of grand stories, the new ideologies, like the cult of efficiency, had unobtrusively slipped in to occupy the vacuum.

Cost-cutting is very important, but not at the cost of community. We had political leaders who believed that anything good for business was great for the State and who spat venom at community concerns, labelling them as anti-Victorian. Initiative and commitment in business shoud be lauded. But while business is desperately needed to create wealth, it is not the same as government. The lines between the two must not become blurred. The rash of ethics courses that sprang up as an antidote to the 'greed is good' motif of the entrepreneurial decade teach the vital importance of a clear delineation of business from government.

The Book of Ecclesiastes became the scripture I turned to most during this period. The writer vented his feelings of a world where satiation, boredom and vanity prevailed. I resonated with this, as that is what it felt like. 'You beaut' theories of massive savings gripped the government's imagination and, even when we conclusively demonstrated that their computer modelling of the savings was dubious, they barely paused for breath.

In St Kilda, there were the makings of something different. We had bred communities within the city who did not relate to the government's savings frenzy because they believed in paying for a greater say in their city. Contempt characterised their feelings towards the inaccessibility of State ministers with wall-to-wall minders on mobile phones. They related to local councillors whom they could access directly. To remove these and replace them with unelected bureaucrats in the name of efficiency was not reform. A community rooted in an energising memory and summoned by radical hopes to be just is still a curiosity and a threat in this management culture. This is a community that has protested passionately about the government's arrogance in placing a Grand Prix car race in one of our local parks. Hundreds of locals have been arrested for trying to stop the cutting down of hundreds of trees for this race.

But we were stewing in the belly of the economic-rationalist beast. The dispiriting nature of this time was the inability to think about the role of community when measured against the idol of efficiency. As a council, we were thoroughly committed to efficiency, but supported activities that were community building. To the government's constant pointing towards the marvels of larger cities, decreeing for us all a certain optimum size, we replied that no tourists walk around these on weekends admiring their supposed efficiency, whereas visitors poured into St Kilda because we spent monies on community groups and art in public places, fostered festivals and street parties, and maintained a diverse community through funding minorities.

In a society which regards inefficiency as blasphemy, it is important to protest that the things our culture values most involve stupendous inefficiency. There is the 'inefficiency' of the writer who spends a day looking at the blank sheet before inspiring us with great literature. The 'inefficiency' of time spent building sand-castles with our kids on the beach, or organising street parties that add nothing to the GNP. The 'inefficiency' of a Meals on Wheels worker who chats to the desperately lonely elderly man in his flat when she could more quickly drop the meal and serve others. When management promises us efficiency in removing democracy and identity, we sense that it will be a bland, smooth and tasteless community.

We have become like a people in a magnificent rose garden who have lost their sense of smell. The appeal of bigger, efficient units is fine if married to a vision for a just society. It is that which gives a reason to efficiency—as we know from history, Mussolini made the trains run on time. Lee Kuan Yew has presided over impressive economic growth in Singapore, but Jesuit priests there are gaoled for criticising the abuse of human rights. Where is the debate about what this society of ours will look like? We have developed a national competition policy, but still do not have a national youth employment policy. Making a few richer in the hope that they will dribble out more wealth for the rest is not a national ethic. Yes, there are some major questions to ask of this lofty ideal of a just society.

One anecdote will suffice in clarifying the ironies. An American mother was horrified to discover that an Australian was cutting the birthday cake into twelve equal pieces. She said, 'What are you doing?' and it was explained that there were twelve children at the party and each would get the same sized piece. The Amercian said that was not fair. 'Why do you not ask the children if they all want a piece and what size they want? That is fair.' Notions of fairness are culturally determined. Equality of choice, or equality of outcome, is a difficult issue to debate—but where is the debate happening?

St Kilda is far from being the kingdom of God, but it did have a council which reflected the fighting spirit of the community. It was the spirit of a community that had long welcomed the broken and marginalised and had reason to protect its seat of government.

The battle for St Kilda reflects the larger picture: the struggle to maintain the bonds of community, to share responsibility for the ethos our generation models for the generation to come.

Postscript

1998

It was the battle against council amalgamation in 1994 which brought me to the attention of the media. That occurred at a time when the State Government had embarked upon a rapid dismantling and defunding of advocacy groups. Far fewer voices were being heard in the public domain, for fear of government reprisal; the contracting out of State-funded community services also involved strict confidentiality clauses in contracts, which prohibited speaking out.

This sweet and sour experience in local politics provided a bridge upon which to stand and be heard in public discourse. Much water has swirled under the bridge since then, with fast and furious currents around anti-gambling campaigns, gun debates, the republic, and indigenous issues. These eddies belong to the next narrative. For the moment, this chapter of the story concludes.

As I reflect on the events of my St Kilda years, I see that they were about the interfacing boundaries of faith and experience, which is where personal growth and transformation occur. I have never been attracted to the conventional climes, even though the Church may seem to many a conservative, status-quo institution. I suspect that it is from the edges of the Church that true gospel hope is explored. Likewise, it is from the margins of society that dominant institutions and powerful ideologies must be tested. The question that must be addressed to them is, Whom do they really serve?

My journey has continued to ask the question of power: who gets what they want in this society and how? The dominant economic paradigms are presented as normal and inevitable. Who dares challenge them with an ethic that can accommodate change but is deeply rooted in the common good? Now that the media is owned by basically four transnational corporations worldwide, an alternative social ethic is hardly likely to emerge from that quarter. Similarly, the universities today must produce tradespeople rather than thinkers; their move to vocational outcomes has weakened their social critique. Can the Church be an independent voice in increasingly secular times, or must we continue to look to political parties and platforms for social leadership and alternative hope?

Certainly the collapse of communism and the retreat of the welfare state in most Western countries has precipitated a crisis of ideas. The Left has philosophically imploded with self-doubt as the market has become all conquering. With footloose global capital dictating the shots to a weakened nation state, the best that any government may attempt is a mild taming of the excesses of market forces. The Left appears to be in an intellectual crisis that has made it unable to strongly defend the public realm, or resist the tide of privatisation. The Left lacks the political heart with which to organise any challenge to the bottom-line of economic rationalism.

But the collapse of communism has also become a problem for the Right, exposing the division between social conservatives and economic conservatives. The fault lines have cracked open around issues such as reconciliation, multiculturalism, immigration, the environment—issues that remained out of sight when the common enemy was State socialism.

Much of my work now is dedicated to a renewed vision for community that is the prescription of neither the Right nor the Left. How do we reconstruct a moral society? As I reread my own words in this book I become anxious. Perhaps I've been too certain, too triumphant—even too neat. I certainly do not feel any such confidence now.

Like most people I meet I sense that we are being subverted by an aggressive ethic of competitive individualism which wilfully declares the only ethical duty to society to be whatever is in a person's own best interests. The reworked Henderson poverty-line methodology has revealed the shocking but not surprising fact that in 1998 seventeen per cent of Australians live below the poverty line, five per cent more than in 1975. The moral framework is no longer a society but merely an economy, which has recategorised citizens as customers and where only winners are lauded, and those without spending power become invisible. What ethical resources can we draw upon to halt this swing to the fads of efficiency and restructuring which undermine our family and social institutions? These are questions I want to explore more deeply in my next book.

Cynics abound in our times. It is too easy to give into the social cynicism that declares we are powerless to resist globalisation, wealth inequality and fragmenting communities. Sadly, cynics are usually disillusioned idealists. To many people I seem an idealist. Whilst I agree that much over the past fifteen years has challenged and dented those ideals and their outworking, I intend to keep taking up the cudgel against pure cynicism. It corrodes both hope and the birthing of fresh ideas and possibilities. I want to keep hope alive and nurture the belief that we can build a truly civil and just society. As David Ben Gurion declared, 'Anyone who does not believe in miracles is not a realist.'

Tim Costello
March 1998

Bibliography

Dutney, A., *Food, Sex and Death: A Personal Account of Christianity*, Uniting Church Press, Melbourne, 1993.

Furphy, J., *Such is Life: Being Certain Extracts from the Diary of Tom Collins*, The Bulletin Newspaper Company Limited Publishers, Sydney, 1903.

Johnston, G., *My Brother Jack*, Collins Fontana Books, Great Britain, 1964.

Longmire, A., *The Show Goes On: The History of St Kilda, Volume III, 1930–1983*, Hudson Publishing, Hawthorn, Victoria, 1989.

McKay, H., *Reinventing Australia: The Mind and Mood of Australia in the 90s*, Angus & Robertson, HarperCollins, Sydney, 1993.

Index